• FOODS OF THE WORLD •

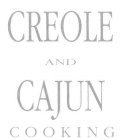

CREOLE
AND
CAJUN
COOKING

For my wife, Kathryn

Acknowledgments

I would like to thank my wife, Kathryn, for her help in writing and testing recipes, especially the breads, cakes, and pies; my daughter, Meghan, and my son, Michael, for helping to test and taste just about everything; Shirley Rideaux, a fine Creole cook, for her advice and encouragement; my agent, Martha Casselman, for her enthusiasm and guidance; and Joyce Oudkerk Pool and David Bowes for the beautifully styled photographs.

Denis Kelly

Thanks to the students at the California Culinary Academy; Michael Bauer; Karen Frerichs; Carol Hacker; Janet Hazen; Gibson Scheid; Jan and Bill Stein; and to Denis for his wonderful recipes.

Joyce Oudkerk Pool

CREOLE
AND
CAJUN
COOKING

Denis Kelly

Photography by Joyce Oudkerk Pool

LITTLE BROWN
AND COMPANY
BOSTON · TORONTO · LONDON

A Little, Brown book

A Kevin Weldon Production
Weldon Publishing is
a division of Kevin Weldon & Associates Pty Limited
Level 5, 70 George Street, Sydney, Australia

This edition first published in 1993

ISBN: 0-316-90604-2
A CIP catalogue record for this book
is available from the British Library

Edited by Patricia Connell and Alice Scott
Food stylist: Daniel Bowe
Printed in Singapore by Kyodo Printing Co (S'pore) Pte Ltd

Little, Brown and Company (UK) Ltd
165 Great Dover Street
London SE1 4YA

CONTENTS

INTRODUCTION

Creole and Cajun cooking, the food of New Orleans and the surrounding countryside, is one of the most vibrant and exciting cuisines in the world today. French in its origin and accents, this spicy and sometimes fiery tradition also embodies elements of Native American, Spanish and African cooking—all brought together by the Creole chefs of New Orleans' great restaurants and the Cajun cooks of the bayous and prairies of southern Louisiana.

New Orleans became part of the United States in 1803 with the Louisiana Purchase, but even today this lively city, tucked into a great bend in the Mississippi just up from the Gulf of Mexico, has a decidedly French flavour. From the rollicking bars and crowded restaurants of the Vieux Carré, or French Quarter, to the quiet and stately antebellum mansions of the Garden District, the city has a Gallic passion for food.

The Creole cooks of New Orleans created a sophisticated and complex cuisine that blends French techniques with local products and traditions. (A Creole is a person born in Louisiana but of French origin). After years of French rule, New Orleans became a Spanish city in the 1760s; Creole cooking relies heavily on ingredients that the Spanish introduced from Mexico, among them tomatoes and peppers (capsicums). Indian tribes such as the Choctaws and Opelousas contributed native ingredients such as filé powder, a blend of ground sassafras bark and thyme used to thicken gumbos and stews. Black Americans, originally brought as slaves from West Africa, did most of the cooking, both in the home and in restaurants. These talented and usually anonymous cooks contributed much to Creole cuisine, including okra (in West African dialects, *n'gombo*), which gave its name to gumbo, the ubiquitous and often fiery stew of seafood, meat and peppers so popular in the region.

Cajun cooking is the earthy, flavourful and sometimes fiery cooking of the southern Louisiana countryside. Cajuns, the French-speaking farmers, fishermen and merchants of such towns as Breaux Bridge and Napoleonville, Lafayette and New Iberia, came to Louisiana as exiles after the English conquest of Canada in the eighteenth century. Most of the new settlers originated in Acadia, which the English later named Nova Scotia, and came to be called Acadians or Cajuns.

Over the years they created a hearty style of cooking similar to, but distinct from, the more "citified" Creole cooking of New Orleans. Cajun cooking uses the products of the bayous and rivers, thickets and canebrakes of rural Louisiana. Lobster or "mudbugs", for example, are one of the most popular Cajun foods, whether heaped up on newspapers at a lobster boil (see page 35) or in spicy and savoury lobster étouffée (see page 38).

Cajun cuisine relies heavily on peppers (capsicums) of every kind. Tabasco sauce from Avery Island, chillies from mild to mouth-searing, green and red peppers, cayenne, paprika, black pepper and white pepper are all used with gusto and abandon by Cajun cooks. In fact, many cooks mix up a special blend of peppers and spices to flavour their favourite dishes: our Cajun spice mix (see page 9) is a good example, and many commercial Cajun flavouring mixes can be found.

One of the mainstays of both Creole and Cajun cooking is the roux made of oil and flour that thickens and flavours soups, stews and gumbos. Most recipes from the region begin with the words "Make a roux...", and this dark, nutty blend of oil and flour provides one of the cuisine's integral flavour. Cooked and stirred in a black iron frypan to the right level of colour and flavour—"blonde roux", "peanut butter roux", "brown roux", "black roux" describe stages in cooking—the mixture contributes flavour, colour and texture to many dishes. Our section on Creole and Cajun basics begins with making a roux (see page 8), which will guide you through the techniques necessary to produce this essential element of the cooking style. We also describe a way to make roux in a microwave that can shorten and simplify the process. Many Creole and Cajun cooks make up large quantities of each type of roux in advance. Roux stores well and is easily reheated—a real convenience in making many of the recipes in the book.

You might find ingredients listed that are not available in your area, although we try to provide substitutes whenever possible. You can follow the examples of Creole cooks and adapt local products.

New Orleans and southern Louisiana have always been a great meeting ground of cultures—French, Spanish, Indian, Black (and later Irish, German and Chinese)—and the region's cooking is a wonderful amalgam of flavours and tastes. Much of the excitement of Creole and Cajun cooking lies in its adaptability and creativity. Use the recipes that follow as guidelines to learn the techniques and flavours of this lively cuisine, and then change them as you will, using local products and seasonings. Creole and Cajun cooking is adventurous above all—so experiment, be creative, and *laissez les bons temps rouler.*

MAKING A ROUX

One of the mainstays of Creole and Cajun cooking, roux is used to flavour, thicken and colour many dishes. It is basically a blend of oil and flour, cooked in a heavy frying pan until it reaches the colour and flavour desired by the cook. The key to a successful roux is to use a good, heavy iron saucepan that will maintain a steady heat, and to stir the mixture constantly as it cooks. Stirring keeps the roux from burning, which is a real possibility if you use too high a heat or are inattentive.

The proportion of oil to flour varies from cook to cook, but in general it is roughly equal. If you find you like a smooth and lighter roux, use more oil; if you prefer a thicker, grainier roux, use more flour. Proportions also seem to vary depending on the oil used, the moisture content of the flour, the type of saucepan and maybe even the weather. Vary the amounts of oil and flour to suit yourself; generally you want a smooth paste about the consistency of thick cream.

Roux keeps very well in the refrigerator, and many cooks make at least a double recipe of roux when they cook up a gumbo. Just put the cooled roux in a bowl and cover with plastic wrap, pressing the wrap down onto the surface. Don't worry if oil separates out. This is normal, and even helps when you reheat the roux. Pour a little of the separated oil into the saucepan and reheat the roux in it.

NOTE: Be careful when preparing roux—use a long-handled wooden spoon and avoid getting any on your skin. Chef Paul Prudhomme, of K-Paul's, the renowned New Orleans restaurant, refers to roux as "Cajun napalm", and he's not really exaggerating.

For a small recipe: 1/4 cup/2 fl oz/60 ml vegetable oil
1/3 cup/1 1/2 oz/40 g plain flour
For a medium recipe: 1/2 cup/4 fl oz/125 ml vegetable oil
2/3 cup/3 oz/85 g plain flour
For a large recipe: 1 cup/8 fl oz/250 ml vegetable oil
1 1/3 cups/5 1/2 oz/165 g plain flour

1. Heat the oil in a heavy frying pan over a medium high heat until hot, about 350°F/180°C. A bit of flour scattered on top should sizzle. Carefully stir in the flour, sprinkling it on top of the oil and stirring constantly with a long-handled wooden spoon.

2. When the flour and oil have mixed into a smooth paste, reduce heat to medium and stir the roux constantly as it cooks.

3. Within 5–10 minutes it will take on a light golden colour; at this stage it is called a "blonde roux", and is used to make gravies for pork chops or cream sauces for fish and vegetables. From this point the roux can be used or refrigerated for later use.

4. For the darker mixture preferred by most Creole and Cajun cooks, keep stirring and cooking the roux over medium heat. It will produce a wonderfully nutty aroma and flavour as it browns.

5. After 10–15 minutes of stirring and cooking, the roux should be a deep golden brown; this is called "peanut butter roux" and is used in many chicken and seafood dishes. After another 10–15 minutes or so of cooking and stirring, the roux takes on a deep brown colour and is called "brown roux", most often used in gumbos and stews. Further cooking produces a "black roux", which many Cajun cooks swear by. It is a bit tricky to judge, however, as care must be taken not to burn the roux at this point.

6. Microwave Roux: Stir the oil and flour together into a smooth paste and put in a large microwave dish or bowl. Microwave for 5 minutes at full power. Remove and stir thoroughly. Microwave for 5 minutes more, remove and stir again, observing the colour—the roux should be light gold or "blonde" at this point. Continue the process until the roux reaches the desired colour, microwaving and stirring at 2–4 minute intervals; shorten the intervals as the roux darkens to avoid burning. Blonde roux should take about 10 minutes total, peanut butter roux about 12–15 minutes and brown roux 18–20 minutes.

CAJUN SPICE MIX

Makes about 1 cup/4 oz/125 g

This peppery spice mix flavours Cajun and Creole sauces, gumbos, jambalaya and many seafood, chicken or meat dishes. Add to marinades, salad dressings and mayonnaise for a bit of Cajun spice. Care should be taken when browning meat, poultry or fish that has been seasoned with a spice mix; most contain paprika, which can burn easily. Don't let the heat get too high, and regulate it as you go.

$^1/_2$ cup/2 oz/60 g paprika
$^1/_4$ cup/1 oz/30 g black pepper
$1^1/_2$ tablespoons or more cayenne
2 tablespoons garlic powder
2 tablespoons onion powder

Combine the spices thoroughly and store in a closed jar in a cool, dry place. Add more cayenne if you want a hotter mix. Use within a month for maximum flavour.

SEAFOOD/FISH STOCK

Makes about 8 cups/2 qt/2 l

Fish stock is easy to make, and adds flavour to soups and gumbos. If you are using prawns or fish in the dish, just cook up the prawn shells and fish trimmings as described below. You can also freeze prawns, lobster and crab shells and fish trimmings for later use in stock. A good substitute is clam juice, although this can be a bit salty, so adjust your recipe accordingly. You can also use chicken stock in place of fish stock, although it produces a slightly different flavour in the finished dish.

8–10 cups/2–2¹/₂ qt/2–2.5 l cold water
2–3 cups/8–12 oz/250–375 g prawn, crab and/or lobster shells or
2–3 cups/8–12 oz/250–375 g trimmings and bones from non-oily fish
1 large onion (unpeeled), quartered
2 garlic cloves (unpeeled), crushed
2 medium carrots, coarsely chopped
1 celery stalk, coarsely chopped
1 teaspoon dried thyme or 2 teaspoons chopped fresh
1 teaspoon dried marjoram or 2 teaspoons chopped fresh
1 bay leaf
1 teaspoon Cajun Spice Mix (page 9)
3 whole peppercorns
salt and pepper

1. In a stockpot or large saucepan combine the water and seafood shells or fish trimmings and bring to the boil. Skim off and discard foam.

2. Add the vegetables, herbs and spices, and simmer the stock gently for 1 hour. Taste for seasoning.

3. Strain and cool stock; refrigerate. Use within two days or freeze for later use in gumbos, chowders, soups and bouillabaisse.

HOT PEPPER PECANS

These spicy nuts are great by themselves as an appetiser or party snack, but can also be used as an accent in salads (see Spinach and Hot Pepper Pecan Salad, page 79) and sauces (see Sauce Meunière with Hot Pepper Pecans, page 46).

1 lb/500 g shelled pecans or other nuts
2 tablespoons vegetable oil
1 tablespoon Cajun Spice Mix (page 9)
$^1/_4$ teaspoon or more cayenne
$^1/_4$ teaspoon black pepper
$^1/_4$ teaspoon white pepper
2 teaspoons salt

1. Preheat oven to 375°F/190°C/Gas 5. Toss the pecans in the oil to coat thoroughly. Mix the spices and salt together and add to the pecans, tossing thoroughly to make sure the spice mixture is evenly distributed.

2. Spread the nuts on a biscuit tray or shallow baking pan and roast for 15 minutes. Cool before serving. The nuts can be stored for up for 2 weeks in a jar or covered bowl.

AUBERGINE PÂTÉ

Serves 8–10 as an appetiser

2 tablespoons olive or vegetable oil
2 aubergines (eggplants)
6 garlic cloves, finely chopped
$^1/_2$ onion, finely chopped
$^1/_2$ red pepper (capsicum), seeded and finely chopped
$^1/_2$ green pepper (capsicum), seeded and finely chopped
1 teaspoon dried oregano
1 tablespoon Cajun Spice Mix (page 9)
$^1/_4$ cup/$^1/_2$ oz/15 g chopped parsley
$1^1/_2$ teaspoons salt
$^1/_4$ teaspoon black pepper
1 cup/8 fl oz/250 ml tomato purée
$^1/_4$ teaspoon Tabasco or other hot pepper sauce
$^1/_2$ cup/4 fl oz/125 ml olive or vegetable oil

1. Preheat oven to 450°F/230°C/Gas 8. Rub 2 tablespoons oil on the aubergines, pierce in a few places with a sharp knife and roast in the oven until soft, about 30–40 minutes. Cool.

2. Peel the aubergines and chop coarsely in a food processor or by hand. Mix thoroughly with all remaining ingredients except the oil. Heat the oil in a large frying pan over medium heat and sauté the mixture for 5 minutes, stirring often.

3. Preheat oven to 350°F/180°C/Gas 4. Place the aubergine mixture in a large soufflé dish or casserole and bake for 30 minutes. Cool and serve with crackers or French bread.

SAUCE REMOULADE

Makes 1¹/₂ cups/12 fl oz/375 ml

This flavourful mayonnaise is delicious on prawns, crabcakes or other seafood. Remoulade sauce will last for up to a week in the refrigerator. It does not freeze well.

1 egg
¹/₄ cup/2 fl oz/60 ml Creole or other whole-grain mustard
1 teaspoon Cajun Spice Mix (page 9)
¹/₄ cup/1 oz/30 g chopped spring (green) onions, including green tops
¹/₄ cup/¹/₂ oz/15 g chopped parsley
1 teaspoon Worcestershire sauce
¹/₄ teaspoon or more Tabasco or other hot pepper sauce
1 teaspoon salt
1 cup/8 fl oz/250 ml vegetable oil

1. Combine all ingredients except the oil in a blender or food processor and pulse once or twice to mix thoroughly.

2. With the machine running, add the oil in a slow, steady stream, blending until the sauce is smooth and creamy. Taste for salt and Tabasco. Serve immediately or refrigerate for later use.

NOTE: If you prefer not to eat raw egg, this can also be made using commercial mayonnaise. Blend all the ingredients except the egg, salt, and vegetable oil with 1 cup/8 fl oz/250 ml good-quality bottled mayonnaise.

PRAWN REMOULADE

Serves 6 as an appetiser

1 tablespoon salt
1 lemon, quartered
1 onion, quartered
3 qt/3 l water
1 lb/500 g large raw prawns, peeled and deveined
2 bunches watercress or 1 head lettuce, shredded
1 recipe Sauce Remoulade (page 13)
chopped parsley
lemon wedges

1. Combine the salt, lemon and onion in water in a large saucepan and bring to the boil. Add the prawns and cook for 3–5 minutes or until they are firm and pink but not overdone. Cool on ice or under running water; refrigerate.

2. Arrange the watercress or lettuce in individual serving dishes or on a platter and place the prawns on top, 4–6 per serving. Spoon Sauce Remoulade over the prawns, sprinkle with parsley and garnish with lemon wedges. Serve any extra sauce on the side.

TOMATO LIME CHILLI SAUCE

Makes about 3 cups/24 fl oz/750 ml

This spicy sauce is delicious on seafood, fish or chicken, and also serves as a tasty dip for raw vegetables.

1 cup/8 fl oz/250 ml tomato sauce or purée
1¹/₂ cups/12 fl oz/375 ml chopped fresh tomatoes with juice
juice of 1 lime
¹/₂ or more jalapeño or other hot fresh chilli, seeded and finely chopped
¹/₂ cup/2 oz/60 g chopped spring (green) onions with tops
¹/₄ cup/¹/₂ oz/15 g chopped parsley
1 tablespoon Southern Comfort, peach brandy, or Triple Sec
¹/₄ teaspoon cayenne
¹/₄ teaspoon or more Tabasco or other hot pepper sauce
1 teaspoon or more salt
¹/₄ teaspoon black pepper
sliced lime

1. Combine all ingredients except the sliced lime in a mixing bowl, and refrigerate for an hour or two before using.

2. Transfer the sauce to a serving bowl and garnish with lime slices.

PRAWNS IN TOMATO LIME CHILLI SAUCE

Serves 6 as an appetiser

1 lb/500 g large prawns (allow 4–5 per person)
½ recipe Spices for Prawn or Crab Boil (page 35), optional
10 cups/2½ qt/2.5 l water
1 cup/8 fl oz/250 ml white wine
1 small onion, quartered
1 lemon, quartered
1 tablespoon salt
6 large romaine (cos) lettuce leaves
1 recipe Tomato Lime Chilli Sauce (page 15)
sliced lime
Tabasco or other hot pepper sauce

1. Peel and devein prawns, leaving tails attached. Tie up optional spices in a small piece of cheesecloth. Bring the water to the boil and add the wine, optional spices, onion, lemon and salt. Lower heat and simmer uncovered for 10 minutes. Add prawns and cook over medium heat for 4–5 minutes or until pink and firm. Remove and cool.

2. Place romaine leaves on individual plates or a platter and arrange 4–5 prawns down the centre of each leaf. Spoon the sauce over and garnish with lime slices. Serve more sauce, lime slices and Tabasco on the side.

BARBECUED PRAWNS

Serves 6 as an appetiser

These are not "shrimp on the barbie", but a delicious way to cook prawns with plenty of garlic—most likely a dish created by New Orleans's large Italian population. The optional barbecue sauce, while not traditional, adds an extra dimension of flavour.

2 oz/60 g salted butter
$^1/_4$ cup/2 fl oz/60 ml vegetable oil
8 garlic cloves, finely chopped
1 tablespoon Cajun Spice Mix (page 9)
1 tablespoon chopped fresh tarragon or 1$^1/_2$ teaspoons dried
$^1/_4$ teaspoon cayenne
juice of 1 lemon
$^1/_2$ cup/4 fl oz/125 ml white wine or light beer
$^1/_2$ teaspoon salt
$^1/_4$ teaspoon black pepper
1 lb/500 g large raw prawns in the shell or peeled and deveined
$^1/_2$ cup/4 fl oz/125 ml Cajun Barbecue Sauce (page 65), optional
Tabasco or other hot pepper sauce

1. Preheat oven to 450°F/230°C/Gas 8. In an ovenproof frying pan, melt the butter in the oil over medium heat. Add all remaining ingredients except prawns and barbecue sauce, stir well and cook over medium heat for 5 minutes. Add the prawns and cook for 3–4 more minutes, stirring often. Place the pan, uncovered, in the oven for 10 minutes or until prawns are pink and firm and the sauce is bubbly.

2. Stir in the optional Cajun Barbecue Sauce and serve.

LOUISIANA CRABCAKES

Serves 6–8 as an appetiser

Accompany these with Sauce Remoulade (page 13) or Tomato Lime Chilli Sauce (page 15).

1 lb/500 g cleaned crabmeat
$^1/_4$ cup/1 oz/30 g finely chopped spring (green) onions
3 garlic cloves, finely chopped
$^1/_2$ red pepper (capsicum), seeded and finely chopped
$^1/_4$ cup/$^1/_2$ oz/15 g finely chopped parsley
1 teaspoon dried thyme or 2 teaspoons chopped fresh
1 tablespoon Cajun Spice Mix (page 9)
$^1/_4$ teaspoon or more Tabasco or other hot pepper sauce
$^1/_4$ teaspoon or more cayenne
1 teaspoon Worcestershire sauce
$^1/_4$ cup/2 fl oz/60 ml tomato purée or tomato sauce
$1^1/_2$ cups/6 oz/175 g or more dry bread or cracker crumbs
2 eggs, lightly beaten
1 teaspoon salt
$^1/_4$ teaspoon black pepper
finely ground cornmeal or flour
vegetable oil for frying

1. In a large bowl mix all ingredients except the cornmeal or flour and vegetable oil, using enough bread or cracker crumbs to hold the mixture together well. Shape into patties about 4 inches/10 cm in diameter and 1 inch/25 mm thick. Coat each cake in cornmeal or flour. Refrigerate until cooking time.

2. Pour enough oil into a large frying pan to come halfway up the crabcakes. Heat over medium high heat until the oil reaches about 350°F/180°C. Test oil by tossing in a cube of bread; it should sizzle and brown, but not burn. Fry the cakes in batches, turning once as they brown, about 3–5 minutes on each side. Drain on paper towels.

OYSTERS ROCKEFELLER

Serves 4 as an appetiser

This dish, a specialty of Antoine's in New Orleans, boasts a sauce "as rich as Rockefeller". The Rockefeller butter is also delicious on baked fish (see Fillet of Sole Rockefeller, page 47) and on grilled seafood or poultry. It can be saved in the refrigerator for later use.

$^1/_2$ cup/4 oz/125 g chopped cooked spinach (fresh or frozen),
thoroughly drained and squeezed dry
$^1/_2$ cup/1 oz/30 g chopped fresh parsley
$^1/_2$ cup/2 oz/60 g finely chopped spring (green) onions with tops
1 teaspoon Cajun Spice Mix (page 9)
$^1/_4$ teaspoon cayenne
2 tablespoons chopped fresh tarragon or 1 tablespoon dried
juice of $^1/_2$ lemon
2 tablespoons Pernod
$^1/_2$ teaspoon salt
8 oz/230 g salted butter, softened
24 large oysters on the halfshell
rock salt (optional)

1. To make Rockefeller butter: Combine all ingredients except the oysters, butter and rock salt in a food processor and pulse once or twice to mix thoroughly. Add the butter in chunks, and process to blend well.

2. Preheat oven to 450°F/230°C/Gas 8. Arrange the oyster shells in a roasting pan, on a bed of rock salt if desired, and put a tablespoon of the Rockefeller butter on top of each oyster.

3. Bake for 10–15 minutes or until the oysters plump up and the sauce is sizzling. Serve the oysters from the pan or arrange on individual plates.

OYSTERS DIABLE

Serves 4 as an appetiser

Diable butter can be chilled and saved for later use. It is also delicious when baked with scallops or prawns, or on grilled or poached fish or chicken (see Grilled Sea Bass Diable, page 42).

$^1/_2$ red pepper (capsicum), seeded and finely chopped
2 garlic cloves, finely chopped
1 tablespoon Cajun Spice Mix (page 9)
$^1/_2$ teaspoon cayenne
1 teaspoon Creole or other whole-grain mustard
juice of $^1/_2$ lemon
2 tablespoons red wine vinegar
$^1/_2$ teaspoon salt
8 oz/230 g salted butter, softened
24 large oysters, shucked, shells and juice reserved
rock or Kosher salt (optional)

1. To make Diable butter: Combine all ingredients except the oysters, butter and rock salt in a food processor and pulse once or twice to mix thoroughly. Add the butter in chunks, and process to blend well.

2. Preheat oven to 450°F/230°C/Gas 8. Arrange the oysters in a roasting pan, on a bed of rock or Kosher salt if desired, and put a tablespoon of the Diable butter on top of each oyster.

3. Bake for 10–15 minutes or until the oysters plump up and the sauce is sizzling. Serve the oysters from the pan or arrange on individual plates.

CAJUN FRIED CHICKEN STRIPS

Serves 6 as main course, 8–10 as an appetiser

Serve as an appetiser or party snack with a spicy sauce such as Sauce Piquante (page 51), Sauce Remoulade (page 13) or Tomato Lime Chilli Sauce (page 15). Cajun Chicken Strips also make a delicious lunch or light dinner with Plaquemine Parish Potato Salad (page 86) and Spinach and Hot Pepper Pecan Salad (page 79).

6 chicken breasts, boned, skinned and cut into
$^1/_2$ x 4 inch/1 x 10 cm strips

Follow directions for Cajun Fried Chicken (page 48), substituting chicken strips for pieces. Cut frying time in half, turning strips often, and check when cooked by cutting into a strip. Drain on paper towels before serving.

SEAFOOD FILÉ GUMBO

Serves 6–8

$^1/_2$ cup/4 fl oz/125 ml vegetable oil
$^2/_3$ cup/3 oz/85 g plain flour
1 onion, chopped
1 green pepper (capsicum), seeded and chopped
4 garlic cloves
$^1/_2$ cup/2 oz/60 g chopped celery
8 cups/2 qt/2 l fish or chicken stock
2 cups/16 fl oz/500 ml chopped tomatoes with juice
$^1/_2$ cup/4 fl oz/125 ml dry sherry
2 tablespoons Cajun Spice Mix (page 9)
$1^1/_2$ teaspoons dried thyme or 1 tablespoon chopped fresh
2 bay leaves
1 tablespoon Worcestershire sauce
$^1/_2$ teaspoon Tabasco or other hot pepper sauce
1 teaspoon salt
$^1/_4$ teaspoon black pepper
1 lb/500 g raw prawns, peeled and deveined
24 oysters, shucked, with juice
1 lb/500 g cleaned crabmeat
$^1/_4$ cup/1 oz/30 g chopped spring (green) onions with tops
$^1/_4$ cup/$^1/_2$ oz/15 g chopped parsley
2 tablespoons filé powder
cooked rice

1. Make a peanut butter roux (see "Making a Roux", page 8) with the oil and flour in a large pot, or reheat 1 cup/8 oz/250 g prepared roux. Stir in the onion, pepper, garlic and celery and cook for 3–5 minutes over medium high heat. Add the stock, tomatoes, sherry, spice mix, herbs, Worcestershire sauce, Tabasco, salt and pepper. Stir well and cook over medium low heat for 20–30 minutes, stirring occasionally. Add more stock if the gumbo seems too thick.

2. Add the prawns and cook for 3–5 minutes. Add the oysters and crabmeat and cook for another 3–4 minutes. Remove gumbo from heat and stir in the spring onions, parsley and filé powder just before serving. Serve in soup bowls over mounds of rice with more filé powder and Tabasco on the side.

CRAB AND PRAWN GUMBO

Serves 6–8

$^1/_4$ cup/2 fl oz/60 ml vegetable oil
$^1/_3$ cup/1$^1/_2$ oz/40 g plain flour
1 onion, chopped
1 green pepper (capsicum), seeded and chopped
$^1/_2$ cup/2 oz/60 g chopped celery
8 cups/2 qt/2 l fish or chicken stock
2 cups/16 fl oz/500 ml chopped tomatoes with juice
1$^1/_2$ tablespoons Cajun Spice Mix (page 9)
1$^1/_2$ teaspoons dried thyme or 1 tablespoon chopped fresh
1 teaspoon dried basil or 2 teaspoons chopped fresh
2 bay leaves
$^1/_2$ teaspoon Tabasco or other hot pepper sauce
1 tablespoon Worcestershire sauce
1 teaspoon salt
$^1/_4$ teaspoon black pepper
1 lb/500 g sliced okra, fresh or frozen
6 small or 4 large crabs, cooked, cleaned and cracked
1 lb/500 g raw prawns, peeled and deveined
$^1/_2$ cup/2 oz/60 g chopped spring (green) onions with tops
$^1/_4$ cup/$^1/_2$ oz/15 g chopped parsley
cooked rice

1. In a large saucepan over medium heat, make a peanut butter roux (see "Making a Roux", page 8) with the oil and flour, or reheat 1 cup/8 oz/250 g prepared roux. Add the onion, green pepper and celery and cook for 3–4 more minutes, stirring occasionally.

2. Add the stock, tomatoes, spice mix, herbs, Tabasco, Worcestershire sauce, salt and pepper and cook for 10–15 minutes. Stir in the okra and cook for 15–20 minutes, stirring occasionally. The okra will thicken the gumbo; if it becomes too thick, add more stock.

3. Add the crabs (leave small crabs whole, break up larger ones) and cook for 10 more minutes. Add prawns and cook 5 minutes. Stir in spring onions and parsley. Serve over mounds of rice in soup bowls.

CHICKEN AND OYSTER FILÉ GUMBO

Serves 6–8

2^1/$_2$–3 lb/1.2–1.5 kg chicken, cut into serving pieces
8 cups/2 qt/2 l water
^{1}/$_2$ cup/4 fl oz/125 ml vegetable oil
^{2}/$_3$ cup/3 oz/85 g plain flour
1 onion, chopped
1 red pepper (capsicum), seeded and chopped
^{1}/$_2$ cup/2 oz/60 g chopped celery
3 garlic cloves, chopped
2 tablespoons tomato paste
2 tablespoons Cajun Spice Mix (page 9)
1^1/$_2$ teaspoons dried marjoram or 1 tablespoon chopped fresh
2 bay leaves
^{1}/$_2$ teaspoon or more Tabasco or other hot pepper sauce
1 tablespoon Worcestershire sauce
1 teaspoon or more salt
^{1}/$_4$ teaspoon or more black pepper
24 oysters, shucked
2 tablespoons filé powder
cooked rice
chopped spring (green) onions with tops for garnish

1. Place the chicken and water in a large saucepan and bring to the boil. Skim off any foam and simmer while you prepare the roux and seasonings.

2. Make a brown roux in a heavy frying pan with the oil and flour (see "Making a Roux", page 8) or reheat 1 cup/8 oz/250 g prepared roux. Stir in the chopped vegetables and tomato paste and cook over medium heat for 3–4 minutes.

3. Add the vegetable mixture to the chicken along with all seasonings except the filé powder. Stir well and cook for 20–30 minutes or until the chicken is tender. Taste for salt, pepper and Tabasco.

4. Add the oysters and cook for 3–5 minutes. Remove from heat and stir in the filé powder. Serve over mounds of rice in soup bowls, garnish with chopped spring onions and offer extra filé powder and Tabasco on the side.

CHICKEN OR RABBIT AND ANDOUILLE GUMBO

Serves 6–8

2¹/₂–3 lb/1.2–1.5 kg chicken or rabbit, cut up
8 cups/2 qt/2 l chicken stock or water
¹/₂ cup/4 fl oz/125 ml vegetable oil
²/₃ cup/3 oz/85 g plain flour
1 medium onion, chopped
4 garlic cloves, chopped
1 red and 1 green pepper (capsicum), seeded and chopped
2 celery stalks, chopped
1 tablespoon Cajun Spice Mix (page 9)
1 teaspoon dried thyme or 2 teaspoons chopped fresh
3 bay leaves
¹/₂ teaspoon or more Tabasco
1 tablespoon Worcestershire sauce
¹/₂ teaspoon black pepper
1 teaspoon salt
2 tablespoons vegetable oil
1¹/₂ lb/750 g andouille or other smoked sausage, such as kielbasa,
cut into 1 inch/2.5 cm rounds
cooked rice
chopped spring (green) onions and parsley for garnish

1. Place the chicken or rabbit in a large saucepan with the water and bring to the boil. Skim off any foam, lower the heat and simmer while you prepare the roux and vegetables.

2. Make a brown roux (see "Making a Roux", page 8) with the oil and flour or heat 1 cup/8 oz/250 g prepared roux in a frying pan. Add the chopped vegetables, stir to coat thoroughly and cook over medium heat for 4–5 minutes. Add the vegetable mixture to the chicken and stir well.

3. Stir in the spice mix, herbs and other seasonings and cook the gumbo, uncovered, over medium heat for 30 minutes or until chicken is tender.

4. Heat 2 tablespoons oil in a frying pan and brown the sausage rounds over medium high heat for 5–7 minutes. Drain the fat. Add the sausages and cook for 5–10 minutes.

5. Serve the gumbo over mounds of rice in soup bowls. Garnish with chopped spring onions and parsley.

GUMBO Z'HERBES

Serves 6–8

2½ lb/1.2 kg mixed greens: chard, mustard, kale, collard, etc.
8 cups/2 qt/2 l chicken stock or water
½ cup/4 fl oz/125 ml vegetable oil
⅔ cup/3 oz/85 g plain flour
1 red onion, chopped
1 red pepper (capsicum), chopped
4 garlic cloves, chopped
2 celery stalks, chopped
2 teaspoons chopped fresh thyme or 1 teaspoon dried
2 bay leaves
1 tablespoon Cajun Spice Mix (page 9)
¼ teaspoon or more Tabasco or other hot pepper sauce
1 tablespoon Worcestershire sauce
1 teaspoon or more salt
¼ teaspoon or more black pepper
cooked rice (optional)

1. Clean the greens thoroughly and chop coarsely. Place in a large saucepan with the stock or water and bring to the boil over high heat. Lower the heat to medium and cook for 30 minutes.

2. Meanwhile, make a brown roux (see "Making a Roux", page 8) with the oil and flour in a large frying pan, or heat 1 cup/8 oz/250 g prepared roux over medium heat. Add the chopped vegetables, stirring to coat, and cook 3–4 minutes. Add the vegetable mixture to the greens and stir.

3. Stir in the herbs, spice mix, Tabasco, Worcestershire sauce, salt and pepper. Taste for seasonings.

4. Simmer the gumbo over medium heat for 15–20 minutes, stirring occasionally. Serve in bowls as a soup or first course, or over rice.

RED BEAN, BOURBON AND MOLASSES SOUP

Serves 4–6

1 lb/500 g dried red beans
1 onion, chopped
1 red pepper (capsicum), seeded and chopped
4 garlic cloves, chopped
1^1/$_2$ tablespoons Cajun Spice Mix (page 9)
2 teaspoons chopped fresh marjoram or 1 teaspoon dried
2 bay leaves
6 cups/1^1/$_2$ qt/1.5 l chicken stock or water
^{1}/$_2$ teaspoon or more Tabasco or other hot pepper sauce
1 tablespoon Worcestershire sauce
^{1}/$_2$ teaspoon or more salt
^{1}/$_4$ cup/2 fl oz/60 ml bourbon whisky
^{1}/$_4$ cup/2 fl oz/60 ml molasses
chopped spring (green) onions and parsley for garnish

1. Prepare beans as directed in the recipe for Red Beans and Rice on page 73.

2. Add all remaining ingredients except the whisky and molasses and simmer over low heat for 2–2^1/$_2$ hours or until beans are tender.

3. Remove 2 cups/16 oz/500 g beans, purée in a food processor or blender and return to the soup. Stir in the whisky and molasses. Add more chicken stock if the soup is too thick; purée more beans if it seems too thin. Cook for 5–10 more minutes. Taste for seasoning. Serve garnished with chopped spring onions and parsley.

GULF COAST SEAFOOD AND CORN CHOWDER

Serves 6–8

2 tablespoons vegetable oil
3 garlic cloves, chopped
1 medium onion, chopped
$^1/_2$ cup/2 oz/60 g chopped celery
$^1/_2$ green pepper (capsicum), seeded and chopped
$^1/_2$ red pepper (capsicum), seeded and chopped
1 tablespoon Cajun Spice Mix (page 8)
1 teaspoon dried thyme or 2 teaspoons chopped fresh
2 bay leaves
3 cups/24 fl oz/750 ml chopped tomatoes and juice
2 cups/16 fl oz/500 ml fish or chicken stock
1 cup/8 fl oz/250 ml dry white wine
$^1/_4$ teaspoon or more Tabasco or other hot pepper sauce
1 teaspoon or more salt
$^1/_4$ teaspoon or more black pepper
1 lb/500 g firm-fleshed white fish fillets such as sea bass, halibut,
snapper or cod, cut into 1 inch/2.5 cm chunks
8 oz/250 g medium prawns, peeled and deveined
2 cups/8 oz/250 g fresh or frozen corn
$^1/_4$ cup/2 fl oz/60 ml sherry
cooked rice

1. Heat the oil in a large saucepan over medium high heat and sauté the chopped vegetables for 2–3 minutes.

2. Add the spice mix, herbs, tomatoes, stock, wine, Tabasco, salt and pepper and stir well. Bring to the boil, reduce heat and simmer uncovered for 30 minutes.

3. Add the fish and simmer 5 minutes. Add the prawns and simmer 3 minutes more. Stir in the corn and cook for 2 minutes or until the fish and prawns are cooked, but not overdone. Taste for seasoning. Add the sherry—dry or sweet, depending on the acidity of the tomatoes.

4. Serve in soup bowls with a ladleful of cooked rice in each bowl. Garnish with chopped spring onions and parsley.

CRAB AND TOMATO BISQUE

Serves 6–8

$^1/_2$ cup/4 fl oz/125 ml vegetable oil
$^2/_3$ cup/3 oz/85 g plain flour
1 red pepper (capsicum), seeded and chopped
1 medium onion, chopped
4 garlic cloves, chopped
2 tablespoons tomato paste
5 cups/40 fl oz/1.2 l fish or chicken stock
3 cups/24 fl oz/750 ml chopped tomatoes with juice
1 cup/8 fl oz/250 ml dry white wine
2 teaspoons chopped fresh marjoram or 1 teaspoon dried
1 tablespoon chopped fresh basil or $1^1/_2$ teaspoons dried
$1^1/_2$ tablespoons Cajun Spice Mix (page 9)
$^1/_4$ teaspoon or more cayenne
$1^1/_2$ lb/750 g cleaned, cooked crabmeat
$^1/_2$ cup/4 fl oz/125 ml heavy cream
$^1/_4$ cup/2 fl oz/60 ml dry sherry
1 teaspoon or more salt
chopped fresh basil for garnish

1. In a large heavy-based saucepan, make a blonde roux with the oil and flour (see "Making a Roux", page 8) or reheat 1 cup/8 oz/250 g prepared roux. Stir in the chopped vegetables and tomato paste and cook for 3–4 minutes, stirring well. Stir in the stock, tomatoes, wine, herbs and spices and simmer over medium low heat for 30 minutes.

2. Cool the bisque and purée coarsely in a food processor or blender. Reheat, stirring well, and add the crabmeat, cream and sherry. Add more stock or tomato juice if the bisque seems too thick. Reheat, stirring, over low heat. Taste for seasonings. Serve topped with chopped basil.

NEW ORLEANS BOUILLABAISSE

Serves 8

Serve this rich fish soup in bowls over toasted French bread slices that have been sprinkled with olive oil and rubbed with garlic.

1 lb/500 g snapper or other firm-fleshed white fish fillets such as ling, cod, ocean perch or gurnard
1 lb/500 g mackerel or other firm-fleshed fish fillets such as halibut, mullet or monkfish
2 tablespoons vegetable oil
1 tablespoon Cajun Spice Mix (page 9)
1 teaspoon each dried thyme, dried tarragon and salt
¼ teaspoon each ground allspice and black pepper
½ teaspoon fennel seed
Broth:
½ cup/4 fl oz/125 ml vegetable oil
⅔ cup/3 oz/85 g plain flour
2 cups/8 oz/250 g sliced leeks, white part only
5 garlic cloves, chopped
½ cup/2 oz/60 g thinly sliced celery
7 cups/¾ qt/1.7 l fish or chicken stock
4 cups/1 qt/1 l chopped tomatoes with juice
2 cups/16 fl oz/500 ml white wine
¼ cup/2 fl oz/60 ml Pernod
1 tbls Worcestershire sauce and ½ tsp Tabasco or hot pepper sauce
½ teaspoon Tabasco or other hot pepper sauce
2 bay leaves and ½ teaspoon saffron
1 teaspoon salt and ¼ teaspoon black pepper
¼ cup/2 fl oz/60 ml olive oil
1 lb/500 g medium prawns, peeled and deveined

1. Cut the fish fillets into 2 inch/5 cm pieces and rub with oil. Blend the spice mix, thyme, tarragon, salt, allspice, pepper and fennel seed and sprinkle over the fish pieces.

2. Make a blonde roux (see "Making a Roux", page 8) with the oil and flour or reheat 1 cup/8 oz/250 g prepared roux. Stir in the leeks, garlic and celery and cook over medium heat for 3–4 minutes, stirring well. Add stock, tomatoes, wine, Pernod, Worcestershire sauce, Tabasco, bay leaves, saffron, salt and pepper. Stir well and cook over medium low heat for 15–20 minutes. Add stock if too thick.

3. Sauté the fish in olive oil over medium heat for 2–3 minutes, turning until almost done. Add the fish and oil to the broth and stir gently. Add the prawns and cook for 3–5 minutes.

DUCK GUMBO

Serves 6–8

1 tablespoon Cajun Spice Mix (page 9)
$^1/_2$ teaspoon cayenne
$^1/_4$ teaspoon ground cumin
1 teaspoon each dried thyme, dried sage and salt
$^1/_4$ teaspoon black pepper
2 ducks (legs, thighs and boned breasts only; use wings and carcasses for stock)
2 tablespoons vegetable oil
$^1/_2$ cup/1 oz/30 g dried mushrooms
1 cup/8 fl oz/250 ml boiling water
$^1/_2$ cup/2 oz/60 g plain flour
1 onion, chopped
4 garlic cloves, chopped
1 green pepper (capsicum), seeded and chopped
$^1/_2$ cup/2 oz/60 g chopped celery
2 tablespoons tomato paste
6 cups/1$^1/_2$ qt/1.5 l defatted duck or chicken stock
1 cup/8 fl oz/250 ml tomato purée
1 tablespoon each vinegar, Worcestershire sauce and molasses
$^1/_4$ teaspoon Tabasco
2 bay leaves
2 tablespoons filé powder
cooked rice

1. Mix the spices, herbs, salt and pepper in a small bowl and rub all over the duck pieces. Heat oil in a frying pan and brown the duck over medium heat for 5 minutes, turning frequently and regulating the heat to prevent burning. Strain and reserve $^2/_3$ cup/5 oz/150 ml duck fat.

2. Soak the dried mushrooms in the boiling water for 15 minutes. Remove mushrooms and chop coarsely. Strain the soaking liquid to remove grit, and reserve.

3. Make a brown roux (see "Making a Roux", page 8) in a large saucepan with the duck fat and flour, or reheat 1 cup/8 oz/250 g prepared roux. Stir in the chopped vegetables and tomato paste and cook for 3–4 minutes.

4. Stir the stock into the vegetable mixture. Add the mushroom water, mushrooms, tomato purée, vinegar, Worcestershire sauce, molasses, Tabasco, bay leaves and duck pieces and cook for 20–30 minutes. Add stock if sauce is too thick.

5. Add salt and pepper to taste. Remove from heat and stir in filé powder. Serve over mounds of rice in soup bowls. Garnish with chopped spring onions and serve extra filé powder and Tabasco on the side.

CORN AND OKRA SOUP

Serves 6

2 tablespoons vegetable oil
1 lb/500 g sliced okra, fresh or frozen
$^1/_2$ onion, chopped
$^1/_2$ red pepper (capsicum), seeded and chopped
$^1/_2$ cup/2 oz/60 g chopped celery
4 cups/1 qt/1 l chicken stock
2 cups/16 fl oz/500 ml chopped tomatoes with juice
1 bay leaf
$^1/_4$ teaspoon or more Tabasco or other hot pepper sauce
salt and black pepper
2 cups/8 oz/250 g corn kernels, fresh or frozen

1. Heat the oil in a large saucepan and fry the okra over medium high heat, stirring well, for 5–7 minutes or until the ropiness subsides. Add the onion, pepper and celery and cook for 3–4 more minutes over medium heat, stirring well.

2. Add the stock, tomatoes, bay leaf, Tabasco and salt and pepper to taste. Cook for 15–20 minutes over medium low heat, stirring occasionally. Add corn and cook 5 more minutes for fresh, 7–10 if using frozen. Serve at once.

CONSOMMÉ CREOLE WITH PEPPERY CROÛTONS

Serves 6

6–8 cups/1^1/$_2$–2 qt/1.5–2 l rich beef stock (see Le Bouilli or Creole Pot
au Feu, page 62), clarified, strained and defatted (see below)
1 egg white, lightly beaten
2 tablespoons tomato paste (concentrate)
^{1}/$_2$ cup/4 fl oz/125 ml dry sherry
^{1}/$_4$ teaspoon Tabasco or other hot pepper sauce
salt and pepper
Peppery Croûtons (page 34)
Garnish:
finely chopped red pepper (capsicum)
spring (green) onion tops

1. Heat the stock, then remove from heat and whisk in the egg white.
Cool. Strain through a fine mesh strainer or muslin. Refrigerate
overnight. Discard fat.

2. Whisk in the tomato paste, sherry and Tabasco, and taste for salt
and pepper. Heat thoroughly. Serve garnished with Peppery
Croûtons, red pepper and spring onion tops.

PEPPERY CROÛTONS

Makes 2 cups/6 oz/175 g

¹/₄ cup/2 fl oz/60 ml vegetable oil
2 cups/6 oz/175 g French bread cut into 1/2 inch/1 cm cubes
1 tablespoon Cajun Spice Mix (page 9)
1 teaspoon dried thyme
1 teaspoon salt
¹/₄ teaspoon cayenne
¹/₄ teaspoon black pepper

1. Heat the oil in a large frying pan over medium high heat. Brown the bread cubes in the hot oil, stirring often and tossing the pan, for 3–4 minutes. Don't crowd the pan; do them in batches if necessary.

2. While the bread cubes are browning, blend the spice mix, thyme, salt, cayenne and pepper in a large bowl. When bread cubes are browned, add to the spice mixture and toss to coat thoroughly.

3. Use croûtons as garnish in soups (see Consommé Creole, page 33) or salads.

SPICES FOR PRAWN, CRAB OR LOBSTER BOIL

Makes about ¹/₂ cup/2 oz/60 g

2 tablespoons whole black peppercorns
2 tablespoons whole mustard seed
1 tablespoon red pepper flakes
1 tablespoon whole coriander seed
1 teaspoon dill seed
6 bay leaves, crumbled
12 whole allspice
6 whole cloves

Mix spices together and store in a tightly covered jar. Use for boiling prawns, crab, lobster or other seafood. If prawns or lobster are shelled before cooking, it is best to enclose spices in a piece of cheesecloth.

PRAWNS, CRAB OR LOBSTER BOILED IN BEER

Serves 8–10

Serve with dipping sauces, such as melted Diable Butter (page 20), Sauce Remoulade (page 13) or Tomato Lime Chilli Sauce (page 15). And don't forget to offer plenty of cold beer and napkins.

3 qt/3 l water
two 12 oz/355 ml bottles beer
2 tablespoons salt
1 recipe Spices for Prawn, Crab or Lobster Boil (page 35)
1 tablespoon or more Tabasco or other hot pepper sauce
2 lemons, quartered
1 onion, sliced
4 lb/2 kg large raw prawns, unpeeled, or 8–10 fresh crabs, or
6 lb/3 kg whole lobster

1. Combine all ingredients except the seafood in a large saucepan and bring to the boil. Add the seafood and cook prawns for 5–10 minutes or until pink and firm, crab from 15–20 minutes depending on size, and lobster 10–15 minutes. The crab and lobster shells should be reddish, the meat firm and tender.

2. Remove the seafood when done and let cool slightly. Place on big platters or newspaper spread on tables, and let guests peel prawns, crack crabs or pick lobster as they go.

PRAWN STEW

Serves 6

$^1/_2$ cup/4 fl oz/125 ml vegetable oil
$^2/_3$ cup/3 oz/85 g plain flour
1 onion, chopped
4 garlic cloves, chopped
1 green pepper (capsicum), seeded and chopped
3 cups/24 fl oz/750 ml seafood or chicken stock
1 cup/8 fl oz/250 ml white wine
1 tablespoon tomato paste
1 tablespoon Cajun Spice Mix (page 9)
1 tablespoon Worcestershire sauce
$1^1/_2$ teaspoons dried marjoram or 1 tablespoon chopped fresh
$^1/_2$ teaspoon or more Tabasco or other hot pepper sauce
1 teaspoon salt
$^1/_4$ teaspoon black pepper
$1^1/_2$ lb/750 g medium prawns, peeled and deveined
$^1/_2$ cup/2 oz/60 g chopped spring (green) onions with tops
$^1/_4$ cup/$^1/_2$ oz/15 g chopped parsley
cooked rice

1. Make a brown roux (see "Making a Roux", page 8) with the oil and flour in a large, heavy frying pan or reheat 1 cup/8 oz/250 g prepared roux. Stir in the chopped vegetables and cook over medium heat for 3–4 minutes.

2. Stir in the stock, wine, tomato paste, spice mix, Worcestershire sauce, marjoram, Tabasco, salt and pepper and cook over medium low heat for 10–12 minutes, stirring occasionally. Add more stock or wine if the sauce seems too thick. Taste for salt, pepper and Tabasco.

3. Add the prawns, cover and cook for 3–5 minutes or until they are pink and firm but not overcooked. Stir in the spring onions and parsley, and serve over rice.

PRAWN OR LOBSTER ÉTOUFFÉE

Serves 4–6

$^{1}/_{4}$ cup/2 fl oz/60 ml vegetable oil
$^{1}/_{2}$ cup/4 oz/120 g salted butter
2 large onions, chopped
$^{1}/_{2}$ green pepper (capsicum), seeded and chopped
$^{1}/_{2}$ red pepper (capsicum), seeded and chopped
1 cup/4 oz/125 g chopped celery
$1^{1}/_{2}$ tablespoons Cajun Spice Mix (page 9)
$^{1}/_{4}$ teaspoon cayenne
1 teaspoon dried thyme or 2 teaspoons chopped fresh
1 tablespoon Worcestershire sauce
1 teaspoon salt
1 cup/8 fl oz/250 ml fish or chicken stock
1 lb/500 g medium prawns, peeled and deveined, or
1 lb/500 g lobster tails, with fat
$^{1}/_{2}$ cup/2 oz/60 g chopped spring (green) onions with tops
$^{1}/_{4}$ cup/$^{1}/_{2}$ oz/15 g chopped parsley
salt and pepper
cooked rice

1. In a large saucepan with cover, heat the oil and butter over medium heat. Add the onions, peppers, celery, spices, thyme, Worcestershire sauce and salt and cook over medium heat, stirring occasionally, for 10–12 minutes or until the onions are limp and translucent.

2. Add the stock and seafood, cover and simmer for 7–10 minutes or until the prawns or lobster are pink and firm but not overcooked.

3. Stir in the spring onions and parsley, and taste for salt and pepper. Serve over rice.

STUFFED CRAB

Serves 4 as main course, 6 as first course

Sauce Piqûante (page 51), Creole Sauce (page 43), or Tomato Lime Chilli Sauce (page 16) makes a good accompaniment for this.

1 lb/500 g cleaned cooked crabmeat
2 cups/6 oz/90 g soft French bread crumbs
$^1/_2$ cup/2 oz/60 g chopped spring (green) onions, with tops
$^1/_2$ cup/2 oz/60 g chopped red pepper (capsicum)
$^1/_4$ cup/1 oz/30 g chopped mild green chilli
$^1/_4$ cup/1 oz/30 g chopped celery
$^1/_4$ cup/$^1/_2$ oz/15 g chopped parsley
1 cup/8 fl oz/250 ml tomato purée or tomato sauce
$^1/_4$ cup/2 fl oz/60 ml dry sherry
juice of 1 lemon
1 tablespoon Cajun Spice Mix (page 9)
$^1/_4$ teaspoon cayenne
1 teaspoon dried oregano
2 tablespoons Worcestershire sauce
$^1/_4$ teaspoon or more Tabasco or other hot pepper sauce
1 teaspoon or more salt
$^1/_4$ teaspoon black pepper
2 eggs, lightly beaten
vegetable oil or melted butter
grated Parmesan cheese

1. Thoroughly mix all ingredients except the eggs, oil and cheese. Taste for seasoning. Add the eggs and blend well.

2. Preheat oven to 400°F/200°C/Gas 6. Brush 4–6 cleaned crab shells or individual ramekins, or a medium-size (9 inch/23 cm) ovenproof serving dish with oil or butter. Spoon in the crab mixture and top with cheese. Bake for 20–25 minutes or until the top is golden brown. Serve hot.

JAMBALAYA

Serves 6

This popular rice and tomato dish can also be made with chicken, rabbit or turkey (see Chicken Jambalaya, page 50).

$^1/_4$ cup/2 fl oz/60 ml vegetable oil
8 oz/250 g ham, cut into small chunks
1 medium onion, chopped
2 garlic cloves, chopped
1 green pepper (capsicum), seeded and chopped
2 celery stalks, chopped
2 teaspoons chopped fresh thyme or 1 teaspoon dried
1 tablespoon chopped fresh basil or 1$^1/_2$ teaspoons dried
1$^1/_2$ tablespoons Cajun Spice Mix (page 9)
2 cups/14 oz/400 g uncooked rice
2$^1/_2$ cups/20 fl oz/600 ml chopped tomatoes with juice
2 cups/16 fl oz/500 ml or more chicken stock
$^1/_2$ teaspoon or more Tabasco or other hot pepper sauce
1 tablespoon Worcestershire sauce
1 teaspoon salt (less if using canned stock)
1$^1/_2$ lb/750 g raw medium prawns, peeled and deveined
chopped spring (green) onions and parsley for garnish

1. Heat the oil in a large Dutch oven or frying pan with cover. Add the ham and sauté over medium high heat for 3–5 minutes. Add the onion, garlic, peppers and celery and sauté for 3–5 more minutes or until the onion becomes translucent, but pepper is still crunchy. Add the herbs, spice mix and rice and stir thoroughly to coat the rice with oil.

2. Stir in the tomatoes, stock, Tabasco, Worcestershire sauce and salt. Reduce heat, cover and cook over low heat for 20 minutes.

3. Stir in the prawns and add more liquid if the rice looks too dry. Cover and cook until the rice is tender and prawns are pink and firm, another 10–15 minutes. Taste for seasoning. Serve sprinkled with spring onions and parsley.

BLACKENED FISH FILLETS

Serves 6

6 fillets of firm white-fleshed fish such as ling, gurnard, snapper, sea
bass or ocean perch, $^1/_2$ inch/1 cm thick
1 tablespoon Cajun Spice Mix (page 9)
$1^1/_2$ teaspoons salt
$^1/_2$ teaspoon or more cayenne
1 teaspoon dried tarragon
$^1/_2$ teaspoon fennel seed
$^1/_2$ cup/4 oz/120 g butter, melted

CAUTION: THIS PROCESS CREATES A LOT OF SMOKE AND CAN
CAUSE FLAREUPS IN THE PAN. IT IS BEST DONE OUTDOORS ON A
GAS OR CHARCOAL BARBECUE OR IN A KITCHEN EQUIPPED WITH
A HEAVY-DUTY EXTRACTOR FAN.

1. Trim the fillets of any skin or bone. Blend the spice mix, salt,
cayenne, tarragon and fennel seed in a small bowl. Place the butter
in a deep dish.

2. Set a heavy cast iron frying pan on an outdoor grill or on a stove
equipped with a restaurant-style exhaust fan. Turn heat to maximum
and heat the pan for at least 5 and no more than 10 minutes.

3. Dip the fillets in the melted butter, then sprinkle both sides with
the spice mixture. With the exhaust fan on high, cook the fillets in
the preheated pan for 2 minutes on each side or until a dark crust
forms and the fish is cooked through. Serve on a platter with a
spoonful of melted butter over each fillet.

GRILLED SEA BASS WITH DIABLE BUTTER

Serves 4

Particularly appealing served with Cajun Rice Salad (page 81) and Sweet Corn and Okra Salad (page 83).

2 tablespoons vegetable oil
4 fillets of sea bass or other firm white-fleshed fish
1 tablespoon Cajun Spice Mix (page 9)
1 teaspoon dried thyme
$\frac{1}{4}$ teaspoon cayenne
1 teaspoon salt
$\frac{1}{4}$ teaspoon black pepper
$\frac{1}{2}$ cup/4 oz/125 g Diable Butter (page 20)

1. Rub oil over the fillets. Combine the spice mix, thyme, cayenne, salt and pepper in a small bowl, and sprinkle over the fish. Heat griller or prepare charcoal grill; if you are using the grill, also preheat oven to 450°F/230°C/Gas 8.

2. Grill the fish until done, 4–6 minutes per side. Place 2 tablespoons of Diable Butter on each fillet and run briefly under the griller or place in a moderate oven for 3–4 minutes to melt. Serve immediately.

3. To Microwave: Prepare the fish as in Step 1. Place on microwave-safe dish and microwave on High for 2 minutes. Turn the fish over and place 2 tablespoons Diable Butter on each fillet. Microwave on High power for 1–3 more minutes or until done.

CREOLE SAUCE

Makes 4 cups/1 qt/1 l

Creole sauce is delicious on poached or grilled fish and chicken, and with roast chicken, duck or pork. It can also be mixed with rice, pasta or vegetables for a tasty side dish. The sauce will last up to a week covered in the refrigerator.

$^{1}/_{4}$ cup/2 fl oz/60 ml olive or vegetable oil
1 large onion, chopped
3 garlic cloves, minced
1 green pepper (capsicum), seeded and chopped
1 cup/4 oz/125 g chopped celery
3 cups/24 fl oz/750 ml chopped fresh tomatoes or
canned Italian-style tomatoes, with juice
1 teaspoon Cajun Spice Mix (page 9)
1 teaspoon dried thyme or 2 teaspoons chopped fresh
$1^{1}/_{2}$ teaspoons dried basil or 1 tablespoon chopped fresh
$^{1}/_{4}$ cup/2 fl oz/60 ml dry sherry
$^{1}/_{4}$ teaspoon or more Tabasco or other hot pepper sauce
1 teaspoon salt
$^{1}/_{4}$ teaspoon black pepper

1. Heat the oil in a frying pan or saucepan over medium heat and sauté the onion, garlic, pepper and celery until the onion is soft and translucent, stirring occasionally, about 3–5 minutes.

2. Add the tomatoes and their juice along with the spice mix, herbs, sherry, Tabasco, salt and pepper. Cook the sauce over medium heat, stirring occasionally and breaking up the larger tomato pieces for 10–15 minutes or until slightly thickened. Add more sherry or tomato juice if the sauce seems too thick. Taste for salt, pepper and Tabasco.

BAKED SNAPPER IN CREOLE SAUCE

Serves 6

Try this with Green Rice (page 75) or Irish Channel Roast Potatoes (page 76).

6 fillets of snapper or other firm-fleshed fish
2 tablespoons vegetable oil
1 tablespoon Cajun Spice Mix (page 9)
1 teaspoon dried thyme
$1/8$ teaspoon ground allspice
1 teaspoon salt
$1/4$ teaspoon black pepper
1 recipe Creole Sauce (page 43)

1. Preheat oven to 350°F/180°C/Gas 4. Trim the fillets of any skin or bones, and rub with oil. Blend the spice mix, thyme, allspice, salt and pepper in a small bowl and sprinkle on both sides of the fish.

2. Arrange the fillets in a baking dish and spoon Creole Sauce over. Bake uncovered for 15–20 minutes or until the fish flakes easily. Serve immediately.

3. To Microwave: Prepare the fish as in Step 1. Arrange the fillets in a microwave-safe dish and microwave on High for 2 minutes. Turn fish and spoon Creole Sauce over. Microwave on High for 1–3 more minutes or until done.

SAUCE MEUNIÈRE WITH HOT PEPPER PECANS

Makes 2 cups/16 fl oz/500 ml

Serve over grilled or poached fish or with veal, chicken breasts or rabbit.

2 tablespoons butter
2 tablespoons plain flour
1 garlic clove, minced
2 tablespoons finely chopped spring (green) onions
1¼ cups/10 fl oz/300 ml seafood or chicken stock
¼ cup/2 fl oz/60 ml white wine or dry sherry
1 tablespoon Worcestershire sauce
¼ teaspoon cayenne
1 teaspoon salt
2 tablespoons chopped parsley
½ cup/3 oz/90 g Hot Pepper Pecans (page 11), or other roasted nuts, chopped
salt and pepper

1. Melt the butter in a saucepan over medium heat, add the flour and stir constantly to make a light roux, about 2–3 minutes. Stir in the garlic and onion and cook for 1–2 minutes more.

2. Pour in the stock, wine and Worcestershire sauce and whisk until smooth. Add the cayenne, salt, parsley and chopped nuts and cook over low heat for 5–7 minutes, stirring occasionally. Add more liquid if sauce seems too thick. Taste for seasoning.

CATFISH FILLETS MEUNIÈRE WITH HOT PEPPER PECANS

Serves 6

6 catfish (rock turbot) or
other firm white-fleshed fish fillets (about 1^1/$_2$ lb/750 g total)
1 tablespoon Cajun Spice Mix (page 9)
1^1/$_2$ teaspoons dried marjoram
1 teaspoon salt
^{1}/$_4$ teaspoon black pepper
^{1}/$_2$ cup/2 oz/60 g plain flour
1 recipe Sauce Meunière with Hot Pepper Pecans (page 45)
2 tablespoons vegetable oil
Hot Pepper Pecans (page 11),
chopped spring (green) onions and parsley for garnish

1. Trim the fillets of any skin or bones. Stir the spice mix, marjoram, salt and pepper into the flour in a pie dish or flat plate.

2. Make Sauce Meunière with Hot Pepper Pecans or reheat reserved sauce.

3. Heat the vegetable oil in a large frying pan over medium high heat. Dredge both sides of the fillets in the seasoned flour and pan-fry for 3–5 minutes on each side until golden brown. Arrange the fish on a platter and pour the sauce over. Garnish with whole Hot Pepper Pecans and chopped spring onions and parsley.

4. To Microwave: Rub the fillets with oil and sprinkle both sides with spice mix and salt. Arrange on a platter and microwave on High for 2 minutes. Turn the fish, spoon sauce over and microwave on High for 1–2 minutes more or until done. Garnish as above.

FILLET OF SOLE ROCKEFELLER

Serves 4

Try this with Green Rice (page 75).

2 tablespoons vegetable oil
6 fillets of sole, flounder or other white-fleshed fish
1 tablespoon Cajun Spice Mix (page 9)
2 teaspoons dried tarragon
1 teaspoon fennel seed
1 teaspoon salt
$^{1}/_{4}$ teaspoon black pepper
8 tablespoons Rockefeller Butter (page 19)

1. Preheat oven to 350°F/180°C/Gas 4. Rub oil over the fish. Combine the spice mix, tarragon, fennel, salt and pepper in a small bowl and sprinkle over the fillets.

2. Arrange the fish in a baking pan and bake for 10–12 minutes or until it flakes easily. Place 2 tablespoons of Rockefeller Butter on each steak, increase oven to 450°F/230°C/Gas 8 and bake for 2–3 more minutes or until the sauce is bubbling.

3. To Microwave: Prepare fish as in Step 1. Microwave on High for 2 minutes. Turn fish and place 2 tablespoons Rockefeller Butter on each fillet. Microwave 1–2 minutes more or until done.

CAJUN FRIED CHICKEN

Serves 6

1¹/₂ cups/6 oz/175 g plain flour
2 tablespoons Cajun Spice Mix (page 9)
2 teaspoons dried marjoram
1 teaspoon dried sage
1¹/₂ teaspoons salt
¹/₄ teaspoon black pepper
1 egg
1 cup/8 fl oz/250 ml milk
¹/₄ cup/2 fl oz/60 ml cream
2–2¹/₂ lb/1–1.2 kg chicken, cut into serving pieces
2–3 cups/8–16 fl oz/250–500 ml vegetable oil

1. Mix the flour, spice mix, marjoram, sage, salt and pepper in a deep plate. Beat the egg with the milk and cream in a shallow dish or pie plate.

2. Soak the chicken pieces in the milk mixture for 10–15 minutes, turning pieces occasionally so that all are well coated. Pour enough oil into a deep frying pan to come halfway up the chicken pieces and heat over high heat to 350°F/180°C; a little flour sprinkled on top should sizzle at about this temperature.

3. Dredge the chicken in the seasoned flour and shake off excess. Fry over medium high heat, turning often, for 20–30 minutes or until deep golden brown, regulating the heat as necessary to prevent burning. The chicken is done when the meat is no longer pink near the bone and a meat thermometer inserted in the thickest part registers 185°F/85°C. Drain on paper towels.

CHICKEN CREOLE

Serves 6

This easy dish is delicious made either on the stove or in the microwave. Serve it over Green Rice (page 75) or Dirty Rice (page 74).

1 tablespoon Cajun Spice Mix (page 9)
1 teaspoon dried thyme
1 teaspoon salt
$^1/_4$ teaspoon black pepper
$^1/_8$ teaspoon ground allspice
$2^1/_2$–3 lb/1–1.2 kg chicken, cut into serving pieces
2 tablespoons vegetable oil
2 cups/16 fl oz/500 ml white wine
1 recipe Creole Sauce (page 43)

1. Blend the spice mix, thyme, salt, pepper and allspice and sprinkle over the chicken. Heat the oil in a frying pan over medium high heat and brown the chicken pieces for 3–5 minutes. Drain off excess fat.

2. Add wine and Creole Sauce and stir well. Cover and simmer over low heat for 1–1$^1/_2$ hours or until the chicken is tender.

3. To Microwave: Brown the chicken over direct heat as in Step 1. Microwave on High for 7 minutes. Turn the chicken, cover with Creole Sauce and microwave for another 10–12 minutes or until done (a meat thermometer inserted in the thickest part should register 185°F/85°C).

CHICKEN JAMBALAYA

Serves 6

1 tablespoon Cajun Spice Mix (page 9)
1 teaspoon dried marjoram
1 teaspoon dried sage
1 teaspoon salt
$^1/_4$ teaspoon black pepper
6 chicken breasts, boned, skinned and cut into 1 inch/2.5 cm pieces
$^1/_3$ cup/$2^1/_2$ fl oz/80 ml vegetable oil
$^3/_4$ cup/3 oz/90 g chopped ham
1 cup/4 oz/125 g chopped green pepper (capsicum)
1 cup/4 oz/125 g chopped onion
$^1/_2$ cup/2 oz/60 g chopped celery
2 cups/14 oz/400 g uncooked rice
2 cups/16 fl oz/500 ml chicken stock
1 cup/8 fl oz/250 ml dry white wine
1 cup/8 fl oz/250 ml tomato purée or sauce
$1^1/_2$ teaspoons dried basil or 1 tablespoon chopped fresh
1 tablespoon Worcestershire sauce
$1^1/_2$ teaspoons Tabasco or other hot pepper sauce
$^3/_4$ cup/3 oz/90 g chopped spring (green) onions with tops

1. Blend the spice mix, marjoram, sage, salt and pepper in a small bowl and sprinkle over the chicken. Heat the oil in a large saucepan or Dutch oven over medium high heat and brown the chicken pieces on all sides for 3–5 minutes. Remove and reserve. Sauté the ham in the oil for 2 minutes. Add the green pepper, onion and celery and sauté for another 3 minutes, stirring frequently. Add the rice and stir thoroughly until coated with oil.

2. Put in the chicken, stock, wine, tomato purée, basil, Worcestershire sauce and Tabasco and stir thoroughly. Cover, reduce heat to low and cook for 25–35 minutes or until rice is done, adding more chicken stock or water if the rice seems dry. Taste for salt and pepper. Just before serving, stir in the chopped spring onions.

SAUCE PIQUANTE

Makes 4 cups/1 qt/1 l

Sauce Piquante is a spicy addition to poached or grilled fish or seafood. It is also delicious over rabbit, chicken, pork chops, rice or vegetables. The sauce will keep covered in the refrigerator for up to a week.

$^1/_4$ cup/2 fl oz/60 ml olive or vegetable oil
1 medium onion, finely chopped
6 garlic cloves, finely chopped
$^1/_2$ green pepper (capsicum), finely chopped
$^1/_2$ red pepper (capsicum), finely chopped
1–2 hot fresh chillies, seeded and finely chopped
3 cups/24 fl oz/750 ml chopped fresh tomatoes or canned Italian-style tomatoes, with juice
1 teaspoon dried thyme or 2 teaspoons chopped fresh
1 teaspoon dried marjoram or 2 teaspoons chopped fresh
2 bay leaves
2 tablespoons Cajun Spice Mix (page 9)
$^1/_4$ teaspoon cayenne pepper
2 tablespoons red wine vinegar
1 tablespoon Worcestershire sauce
$^1/_4$ teaspoon or more Tabasco or other hot pepper sauce
1 teaspoon or more salt
$^1/_4$ teaspoon black pepper

1. Heat the oil in a frying pan or saucepan over medium heat and sauté the onion, garlic and peppers, stirring occasionally, until the onion is soft and translucent, about 3–5 minutes.

2. Stir in the tomatoes and their juice along with the herbs and spices, vinegar, Worcestershire sauce, Tabasco, salt and pepper. Cook over medium heat, stirring occasionally and breaking up the larger tomato pieces, for 10–15 minutes or until slightly thickened. Taste for salt and pepper, and add more Tabasco if you like a hotter sauce.

CHICKEN OR RABBIT IN SAUCE PIQUANTE

Serves 4-6

Serve this with Dirty Rice (page 74) and Hot Greens with Pot Likker (page 72).

1 young chicken or rabbit, cut into serving pieces
2 tablespoons vegetable oil
1 tablespoon Cajun Spice Mix (page 9)
$^1/_4$ teaspoon cayenne
1 teaspoon dried marjoram
1 teaspoon dried sage
1 teaspoon salt
1 recipe Sauce Piquante (page 51)

1. Preheat oven to 350°F/180°C/Gas 4. Rub the chicken or rabbit pieces with oil. Blend the spice mix, cayenne, marjoram, sage and salt and sprinkle all over the meat. Place in a baking tray and roast for 45 minutes. Cover with Sauce Piqûante and bake for 10–15 minutes more or until done; a meat thermometer inserted in the thickest part should register 185°F/85°C.

2. To Microwave: Rub the meat with the seasoning mixture and brown in oil. Microwave on High for 7 minutes; turn, cover with Sauce Piquante and microwave for 10–12 minutes more or until done.

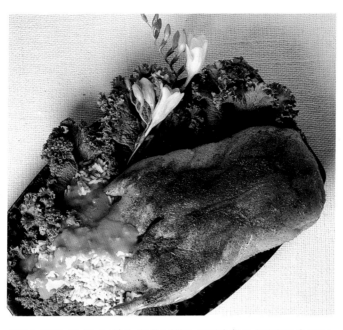

SPICY ROAST DUCK WITH WHISKY PEPPER GRAVY

Serves 6

Save any leftover skin and attached meat for Duck Cracklins and Bitter Greens Salad (page 85).

4–6 lb/2–3 kg duck
1 tablespoon Cajun Spice Mix (page 9)
1 teaspoon dried sage
1 teaspoon salt
$^1/_4$ teaspoon black pepper
1 onion, quartered
4 garlic cloves, crushed
1 celery stalk
Whisky Pepper Gravy (page 54)
Dirty Rice (page 74)

1. Preheat oven to 400°F/200°C/Gas 6. Rub the duck all over with the spice mix, sage, salt and pepper. Place the onion, garlic and celery in the cavity.

2. Roast the duck on a rack in a baking tray for $1^1/_2$–2 hours or until a meat thermometer inserted in the thickest part of the thigh registers 185°F/85°C; prick the skin with a skewer or sharp knife during cooking so the fat can render easily. Pour off the fat as it accumulates, strain and reserve $^1/_2$ cup/4 fl oz/125 ml for gravy.

3. Serve the duck with Dirty Rice, adding the duck livers if you wish, and with Whisky Pepper Gravy.

WHISKY PEPPER GRAVY

Makes 4–5 cups/1–1¹/₄ qt/1–1.2 l

¹/₂ cup/4 oz/125 g duck fat or vegetable oil
²/₃ cup/3 oz/85 g plain flour
1 red pepper (capsicum), seeded and finely chopped
1 jalapeño or other hot green chilli, seeded and finely chopped
1 onion, finely chopped
4 garlic cloves, finely chopped
1 tablespoon tomato paste
1¹/₂ tablespoons Cajun Spice Mix (page 9)
4 cups/1 qt/1 l or more chicken, duck or beef stock
¹/₄ teaspoon or more Tabasco or other hot pepper sauce
2 tablespoons Worcestershire sauce
2 tablespoons vinegar
¹/₄ cup/2 fl oz/60 ml bourbon whisky
2 tablespoons molasses
1 teaspoon or more salt

1. In a large frying pan over medium heat, make a brown roux using the duck fat or vegetable oil and flour (See "Making a Roux", page 8), or reheat 1 cup/8 oz/250 g prepared roux. Stir in the peppers, onion, garlic and tomato paste and cook 3–4 minutes more.

2. Add the spice mix, 4 cups stock, Tabasco, Worcestershire sauce, vinegar, whisky and molasses, stirring well to make a smooth gravy, and simmer for 10–12 minutes over medium low heat. Add more stock if gravy is too thick. Taste for seasonings. Leftover gravy can be kept covered in the refrigerator for up to a week and is delicious on chicken, beef or pork.

BRAISED QUAIL OR BAYOU TECHE

Serves 4

Serve these succulent birds over Dirty Rice (page 74) made from the quail or other poultry livers, or over cooked shell macaroni.

4 quail, game hens, squabs or other small birds
$^{1}/_{4}$ cup/2 fl oz/60 ml vegetable oil
$^{1}/_{3}$ cup/1$^{1}/_{2}$ oz/40 g plain flour
1 onion, chopped
4 garlic cloves, chopped
1 green pepper (capsicum), seeded and chopped
1 mild green chilli, seeded and chopped
1 carrot, chopped
1 celery stalk, chopped
2 cups/6 oz/175 g chopped mushrooms
3 cups/24 fl oz/750 ml tomato purée or crushed tomatoes
12 oz/355 ml bottle dark beer
2 tablespoons molasses
$^{1}/_{2}$ cup/4 fl oz/125 ml or more chicken stock
1$^{1}/_{2}$ teaspoons dried marjoram or 1 tablespoon chopped fresh
2 bay leaves
1 tablespoon Cajun Spice Mix (page 9)
1$^{1}/_{2}$ tablespoons Worcestershire sauce
1 teaspoon salt
$^{1}/_{4}$ teaspoon black pepper

1. In a large heavy-based casserole dish, brown the birds in the oil over a medium high heat. Remove and reserve. Make a brown roux (See "Making a Roux", page 8) with the flour and the oil left in the pan (add more oil if needed for roux). Add all the chopped vegetables except the tomatoes to the roux and cook over medium heat for 3–5 minutes, stirring frequently.

2. Add the tomatoes, beer, molasses, $^{1}/_{2}$ cup stock, herbs, spice mix, Worcestershire sauce, salt and pepper. Stir well and return the birds to the pan. Cover and simmer over low heat for 45 minutes–1 hour, adding stock if sauce seems thick. Taste for salt and pepper.

CAMPFIRE BURGOO OR GAME STEW

Serves 6–8

2–3 lb/1–1.5 kg rabbit, chicken or pheasant, whole or quartered
1 lb/500 g venison or lamb, cut into
1 inch/2.5 cm cubes, fat and gristle removed
1 lb/500 g pork or wild boar, cut into
1 inch/2.5 cm cubes, fat and gristle removed
8 cups/2 qt/2 l chicken stock or water
3 cups/24 fl oz/750 ml chopped tomatoes and juice
1 large onion, chopped
6 garlic cloves, chopped
1 cup/4 oz/125 g chopped celery
3 carrots, sliced
1 lb/500 g new potatoes, quartered
2 bay leaves
1$^1/_2$ teaspoons dried thyme or 1 tablespoon chopped fresh
2 tablespoons Cajun Spice Mix (page 9)
$^1/_2$ teaspoon Tabasco or other hot pepper sauce, or more to taste
1 tablespoon Worcestershire sauce
$^1/_2$ teaspoon red pepper flakes
1$^1/_2$ cups/6 oz/175 g sliced fresh or frozen okra
2 cups/8 oz/250 g fresh or frozen small lima beans
2 cups/8 oz/250 g fresh or frozen corn kernels
1 teaspoon or more salt
$^1/_4$ teaspoon or more black pepper

1. Place all the meats in a large saucepan or Dutch oven, add the stock or water and bring to the boil, skimming off any foam. Add the tomatoes, onion, garlic, celery, carrots, potatoes, bay leaves, thyme, spice mix, Tabasco, Worcestershire sauce and red pepper flakes and simmer, uncovered, for 1$^1/_4$ hours or until the rabbit, chicken or pheasant is tender. Remove, cool and cut meat from the bones. Return the rabbit, chicken or pheasant meat to the pan and simmer 15 minutes.

2. Add the okra, lima beans, corn, salt and pepper and cook 15 minutes more. Taste for salt, pepper and Tabasco.

GRILLADES

Serves 6–8

Perfect with Green Rice (page 75) and Hellfire Biscuits (page 90).

2–3 lb/1–1.5 kg round steak, ¹/₂–³/₄ inch/1–2 cm thick
1¹/₂ tablespoons Cajun Spice Mix (page 9)
1 teaspoon dried oregano
1 teaspoon salt
¹/₂ teaspoon black pepper
¹/₄ cup/2 fl oz/60 ml vegetable oil
¹/₃ cup/1¹/₂ oz/40 g plain flour
¹/₂ onion, chopped
6 garlic cloves, chopped
¹/₂ cup chopped green pepper (capsicum)
¹/₂ cup chopped red pepper (capsicum)
1 cup/8 fl oz/250 ml dry red wine
3 cups/24 fl oz/750 ml chopped tomatoes and juice
1 cup/8 fl oz/250 ml or more beef stock
1 tablespoon Worcestershire sauce
¹/₄ teaspoon Tabasco or other hot pepper sauce
2 bay leaves

1. Trim the round steak of fat and cut into 3 x 5 inch/7.5 x 10 cm pieces. Blend the spice mix, oregano, salt and pepper in a small bowl and sprinkle on the meat.

2. In a large frying pan with cover, heat the oil over a medium heat. Brown the meat pieces on both sides, turning often and regulating heat so they don't burn. Remove and keep warm. Add the flour to the oil remaining in the pan (add more oil if needed) and stir well to make a peanut butter roux (See "Making a Roux", page 8). Stir in the onion, garlic and peppers and cook for 3–5 minutes, stirring occasionally.

3. Add the wine, tomatoes, 1 cup stock, Worcestershire sauce, Tabasco and bay leaves and stir well. Return the beef to the pan with its juices, cover and simmer 1¹/₂–2 hours or until tender; add more stock if sauce is too thick. Taste for salt, pepper and Tabasco.

BEEF EN DAUBE À LA CREOLE

Serves 8

4–5 lb/2–2.5 kg shoulder, round or chuck beef roast, rolled and tied
3 garlic cloves, cut into slivers
2 tablespoons Cajun Spice Mix (page 9)
1 tablespoon dried thyme
$^1/_4$ teaspoon ground allspice
1 teaspoon salt
$^1/_4$ cup/2 fl oz/60 ml vegetable oil
1 onion, chopped
1 green or red pepper (capsicum), seeded and chopped
2 carrots, chopped
3 bay leaves
1 cup/8 fl oz/250 ml red wine
1 cup/8 fl oz/250 ml beef stock
Tabasco or other hot pepper sauce
$^1/_4$ cup/2 oz/60 g Brown Roux (see "Making a Roux", page 8),
optional

1. Poke holes in the roast with a thin knife or skewer and insert the garlic slivers. Blend the spice mix, thyme, allspice and salt and rub all over the beef.

2. Heat the oil in a heavy-based casserole dish over a medium high heat and brown the roast on all sides. Remove the roast and cook the chopped vegetables in the remaining oil for 3–4 minutes or until the onion is translucent.

3. Return the roast to the casserole and add the bay leaves and liquids. Cover and cook over low heat for $1^1/_2$–2 hours.

4. Remove the meat and keep warm. Defat the sauce and taste for seasoning. Serve as is, or thicken by stirring in the roux over medium heat. Alternatively, the sauce can be strained and used in place of beef stock to make Whisky Pepper Gravy (page 54). Slice the meat and spoon the sauce over.

BLACKENED STEAK OR PRIME RIB

Serves 6

6 steaks or slices of prime rib, $^1/_2$–$^3/_4$ inch/1–2 cm thick
1 tablespoon Cajun Spice Mix (page 9)
1$^1/_2$ teaspoons salt
$^1/_2$ teaspoon or more cayenne
1 teaspoon dried thyme
$^1/_2$ cup/4 oz/120 g butter, melted

CAUTION: THIS PROCESS CREATES A LOT OF SMOKE AND CAN CAUSE FLAREUPS IN THE PAN. IT IS BEST DONE OUTDOORS ON A GAS OR CHARCOAL BARBECUE OR IN A KITCHEN EQUIPPED WITH A HEAVY-DUTY EXTRACTOR FAN.

1. Trim the steaks of fat. Blend the spice mix, salt, cayenne and thyme in a small bowl. Place the butter in a deep dish.

2. Set a heavy cast iron frying pan on an outdoor grill or on a stove equipped with a restaurant-style exhaust fan. Turn heat to maximum and heat the pan for at least 5 and no more than 10 minutes.

3. Dip the steaks in the melted butter, then sprinkle both sides with the spice mixture. With the exhaust fan on high, cook the steaks in the preheated pan for 2 minutes on each side or until a dark crust forms and the steaks are medium rare. Serve on a platter with a spoonful of melted butter over each steak.

STEAK VIEUX CARRÉE

Serves 4

1 tablespoon Cajun Spice Mix (page 9)
1 teaspoon dried tarragon
1 teaspoon salt
4 fillet or rib-eye steaks, about 1^1/$_2$ inches/3.5 cm thick
2 tablespoons vegetable oil
^{1}/$_4$ cup/2 oz/60g salted butter
4 garlic cloves, finely chopped
^{1}/$_4$ cup/1 oz/30 g chopped spring (green) onions
2 tablespoons chopped fresh tarragon or 1 tablespoon dried
1 tablespoon Creole or other coarse-grained mustard
^{2}/$_3$ cup/5 fl oz/150 ml cream
^{1}/$_4$ cup/2 fl oz/60 ml Pernod
salt and black pepper
chopped tomatoes and fresh tarragon for garnish

1. Blend the spice mix and dried tarragon in a small bowl. Sprinkle the mixture on both sides of the steaks.

2. Heat the oil in a large frying pan over medium high heat. Pan-fry the steaks 3–5 minutes on each side to the degree of cooking you wish. Remove the steaks from the pan and keep warm while you prepare the sauce.

3. Turn the heat down to medium. Add the butter to the pan and sauté the garlic and spring onions for 2–3 minutes, stirring with a wooden spoon. Stir in the tarragon and mustard. Add the cream and Pernod and heat, stirring well, for 2 minutes more. Serve sauce over the steaks, garnished with chopped tomato and fresh tarragon.

TOURNEDOS SAUCE ESPAGNOLE

Serves 6

This sauce is also delicious on roast beef and grilled pork.

6 tournedos or other small steaks
1 tablespoon Cajun Spice Mix (page 9)
1 teaspoon salt
1¹/₂ tablespoons vegetable oil
¹/₄ cup/1¹/₂ oz/45 g finely chopped andouille or other smoked sausage
2 tablespoons plain flour
2 garlic cloves, finely chopped
¹/₄ cup/1 oz/30 g finely chopped spring (green) onions
¹/₄ cup/1 oz/30 g finely chopped green pepper (capsicum)
1¹/₂ cups/12 fl oz/350 ml beef stock
¹/₄ cup/2 fl oz/60 ml red wine
1 tablespoon tomato paste
1 tablespoon Worcestershire sauce
¹/₄ teaspoon Tabasco or other hot pepper sauce
salt and black pepper
chopped parsley and spring (green) onions for garnish

1. Trim the steaks of fat. Blend the spice mix and salt in a small bowl and sprinkle over the steaks.

2. Heat the oil in a frying pan over medium high heat and brown the sausage for 3–5 minutes, stirring. Remove sausage with a slotted spoon, leaving about 3 tablespoons oil in the pan. Add the flour and make a peanut butter roux (see "Making a Roux", page 8).

3. Add the chopped vegetables and cook over medium heat for 2–3 minutes, stirring well. Stir in all other ingredients except the salt, pepper and garnish and cook over medium heat 5–7 minutes, stirring occasionally. If sauce is too thick, add more liquid.

4. Grill or pan-fry the steaks to desired cooking. Arrange steaks on a platter, pour the sauce over and garnish with chopped parsley and spring onions.

LE BOUILLI OR CREOLE POT AU FEU

Serves 8 with leftovers

The leftover beef can be sliced and heated in Sauce Piquante (page 51), Creole Sauce (page 43) or Cajun Barbecue Sauce (page 65).

5–6 lb/2.5–3 kg beef brisket
8 cups/2 qt/2 l water or to cover
1 large onion, peeled and stuck with 4 whole cloves
8 garlic cloves, crushed
2 celery stalks, cut into 2 inch/5 cm pieces
2 carrots, scraped and cut into 2 inch/5 cm pieces
2 bay leaves
2 teaspoons salt
6 whole peppercorns
4 whole allspice
$1/4$ teaspoon red pepper flakes
Sauce Piquante (page 51)

1. Trim the brisket of excess fat. Cover with water in a large saucepan and bring to the boil. Skim off and discard foam.

2. Add all remaining ingredients and simmer slowly, uncovered, for 2–3 hours or until the beef is tender. Strain stock and reserve for Consommé Creole (page 33) or other uses.

3. Slice the beef across the grain and serve with Sauce Piqûante.

PORK OR VEAL CUTLETS PANÉE WITH SAUCE PIQUANTE

Serves 4

8 slices pork loin or veal cutlets, $^1/_2$ inch/1 cm thick
1 tablespoon Cajun Spice Mix (page 9)
1 cup/4 oz/125 g plain flour
2 eggs
1 teaspoon dried marjoram
1 teaspoon salt
$^1/_4$ teaspoon black pepper
1 cup/4 oz/125 g fine cracker crumbs or dry breadcrumbs
1 recipe Sauce Piquante (page 51)
$^3/_4$ cup/6 fl oz/175 ml vegetable oil

1. Trim fat from the pork or veal cutlets and flatten them slightly with the side of a cleaver. Slash edges in two or three places so they won't curl up when frying.

2. Using three pie plates or flat bowls, blend the spice mix and flour in one; beat the eggs with one teaspoon water in another; and mix the marjoram, salt, pepper and crumbs in the third (omit salt if using salted crackers for crumbs). Heat the Sauce Piqûante in a saucepan and keep warm.

3. Heat the oil to 350°F/180°C in a large frying pan. Dip both sides of each cutlet first in the seasoned flour, then in the egg and then in the crumbs. Fry in the hot oil for 3–5 minutes on a side or until brown and crisp. Drain on paper towels. Serve with Sauce Piquante spooned over the cutlets.

CAJUN MARINADE OR BASTING SAUCE

Makes about 2¹/₂ cups/20 fl oz/300 ml

12 fl oz/355 ml bottle beer
¹/₂ cup/4 fl oz/125 ml vegetable oil
6 garlic cloves, minced
1 tablespoon dry mustard
¹/₄ cup/2 fl oz/60 ml Worcestershire sauce
2 tablespoons Cajun Spice Mix (page 9)
1 teaspoon or more Tabasco or other hot pepper sauce
juice of 1 lemon
1¹/₂ teaspoons salt
¹/₂ teaspoon black pepper

1. Combine all ingredients thoroughly in a bowl or jar. Marinate seafood, chicken, pork or beef in the sauce before grilling and use the sauce to baste food on the grill or in the oven.

2. The sauce will keep refrigerated in a covered jar for up to a week.

CAJUN BARBECUE SAUCE

Makes 10 cups / 2¹/₂ qt / 2.5 l

6 cups/1¹/₂ qt/1.5 l tomato sauce or puréed tomatoes
1 small can (6 oz/175 g) tomato paste
12 oz/355 ml bottle dark beer
1 large onion, finely chopped
8 garlic cloves, finely chopped
1 red pepper (capsicum), finely chopped
1 or more jalapeño or
other hot fresh chilli, seeded and finely chopped (optional)
2 tablespoons Cajun Spice Mix (page 9)
3 bay leaves
2 teaspoons dried thyme
1 teaspoon ground cumin
1 tablespoon mustard powder
¹/₄ teaspoon or more cayenne pepper
2 tablespoons red wine vinegar
juice of 1 lemon
2 tablespoons Worcestershire sauce
¹/₂ cup/6 oz/175 g molasses
¹/₄ cup bourbon whisky (optional)
¹/₂ teaspoon or more Tabasco or other hot pepper sauce
1 teaspoon or more salt
¹/₄ teaspoon black pepper

1. Mix all the ingredients thoroughly in a large stainless steel or enamel saucepan and bring to the boil, stirring well. Reduce heat to low and simmer uncovered for 45 minutes–1 hour, stirring from time to time. Taste for seasoning. This barbecue sauce is traditionally quite hot, but you can adjust the spice level to your taste.

2. Baste grilled or roast meat, poultry and seafood with the sauce for the last few minutes of cooking. Serve more heated sauce on the side.

3. Cajun Barbecue Sauce will last up to two weeks in a covered jar in the refrigerator and also freezes well.

BARBECUED PORK ROAST

Serves 8–10

Irish Channel Roast Potatoes (page 76) and Pickled Corn and Okra Salad (page 83) make perfect accompaniments to this hearty roast.

4–5 lb/2–2.5 kg pork loin roast, boned and tied
2 teaspoons dried sage
$^1/_4$ teaspoon ground cumin
1 tablespoon Cajun Spice Mix (page 9)
1 teaspoon salt
$^1/_4$ teaspoon black pepper
6 garlic cloves, finely chopped
1 cup/8 fl oz/250 ml Cajun Marinade or Basting Sauce (page 64)
1 cup/8 fl oz/250 ml Cajun Barbecue Sauce (page 65)

1. Prepare a Weber or other kettle barbecue for indirect roasting (i.e. not directly over coals) or preheat oven to 350°F/180°C/Gas 4. Mix the sage, cumin, spice mix, salt and pepper in a small bowl. Cut slashes in the pork roast and rub with the spice mixture and garlic, pushing seasonings into the meat wherever possible.

2. Roast in the barbecue or oven about $1^1/_2$–2 hours, or until a meat thermometer inserted in the thickest part of the meat registers 170°F/75°C, basting with the marinade or basting sauce every 15 minutes or so. Baste with Cajun Barbecue Sauce two or three times in the last 30 minutes of cooking, and serve more on the side.

CREOLE PORK CHOPS

Serves 6

6 loin pork chops, 1¹/₂ inches/3.5 cm thick
1 tablespoon Cajun Spice Mix (page 9)
1¹/₂ teaspoons dried sage
1 teaspoon dried marjoram
1 teaspoon salt
2 tablespoons vegetable oil
1 recipe Creole Sauce (page 43)

1. Trim the chops of excess fat and slash the edges so they won't curl while cooking. Blend the spice mix, sage, marjoram and salt and sprinkle over the chops.

2. Preheat oven to 350°F/180°C/Gas 4. Heat the oil over medium high heat in a heavy-based casserole dish, and brown the chops for 3–4 minutes on each side.

3. Drain off fat and cover the chops with Creole Sauce. Cover the pan and bake for 45 minutes or more until a meat thermometer inserted in the chops registers 170°F/75°C.

4. To Microwave: Prepare and brown the chops as in Steps 1 and 2. Arrange the chops in a microwave dish and microwave on High for 8 minutes. Turn and cover with Creole Sauce. Microwave another 8 minutes or until done.

STUFFED ARTICHOKES ATCHIFALAYA

Serves 6 as an appetiser or first course

6 artichokes
1 lemon, sliced
1 onion, sliced
3 bay leaves
2 teaspoons salt
1 teaspoon Tabasco or other hot pepper sauce
2 cups/16 fl oz/500 ml or more water
1 recipe stuffing for Stuffed Crab (page 39)
grated Parmesan cheese
Creole Sauce (page 43), Sauce Piquante (page 51), or
Sauce Remoulade (page 13)

1. Trim the bottoms and tops of the artichokes and rub with lemon. Arrange the artichokes in a steamer rack or colander in a large saucepan and add water to just below the level of the rack. Add the lemon, onion, bay leaves, salt and Tabasco to the water. Bring to the boil, cover and steam for 20–25 minutes.

2. Preheat oven to 375°F/190°C/Gas 5. Prepare the stuffing for Stuffed Crab while the artichokes steam. When they are tender, remove and invert in colander in the sink to drain and cool. Open up the centre of each artichoke and scrape out the choke with a spoon or grapefruit corer. Fill the centres of the artichokes with the crab stuffing and separate the leaves to insert additional stuffing. Sprinkle the tops with grated Parmesan.

3. Place the artichokes on an oiled biscuit tray or in a baking dish and bake 20–25 minutes or until the tops are golden brown. Serve as is, or with Creole Sauce, Sauce Piquante or Sauce Remoulade.

MAQUECHOUX: CORN AND PEPPER SAUTÉ

Serves 6

2 tablespoons vegetable oil
$^{1}/_{2}$ green pepper (capsicum), seeded and chopped
$^{1}/_{2}$ red pepper (capsicum), seeded and chopped
$^{1}/_{2}$ red onion, chopped
1 cup/4 oz/125 g chopped spring (green) onions
4 cups/16 oz/500 g fresh or frozen corn kernels
$^{1}/_{4}$ cup/2 fl oz/60 ml chicken stock
1 teaspoon Cajun Spice Mix (page 9)
1 teaspoon or more salt
$^{1}/_{4}$ teaspoon black pepper

1. Heat the vegetable oil in a large frying pan over medium high heat. Add the peppers and onions and sauté for 3–5 minutes or until the onion is translucent and the peppers are crisp-tender.

2. Stir in the corn, stock and seasonings. Cover and cook over medium heat, stirring occasionally, for 2 minutes more if using fresh corn, 5 minutes if using frozen. The corn should be hot and tender but not overcooked. Serve immediately.

SHIRLEY'S STUFFED PEPPERS

Serves 6 as an appetiser, 3 as a main course

This recipe from Shirley Rideaux, an accomplished Creole cook, is easy, inexpensive and a family favourite. If you prefer the peppers crunchy, bake or microwave for the shorter time cited below. If you like, serve with Creole Sauce (page 43) or Sauce Piquante (page 51).

2 tablespoons vegetable oil
1 lb/500 g lean ground beef
6 garlic cloves, chopped
1 onion, chopped
1 cup/4 oz/125 g chopped spring (green) onions
2 teaspoons Cajun Spice Mix (page 9)
$^1/_2$ jalapeño or other hot green chilli, seeded and finely chopped
1 teaspoon or more salt
2 cups/8 oz/250 g cooked rice
1 egg
3 red or green peppers (capsicums)
grated Parmesan cheese

1. Heat the oil in a large frying pan and brown the beef, stirring well so it breaks up. Pour off fat. Add the garlic and onions and sauté for 3–4 minutes, stirring well. Mix with all other ingredients except the peppers and cheese in a large bowl, and taste for seasoning.

2. Preheat oven to 400°F/200°C/Gas 6. Cut the peppers in half lengthwise and clean out the centres. Blanch the peppers for 2–3 minutes in boiling water; drain and cool. Stuff with the meat mixture.

3. Arrange the peppers on an oiled baking tray and bake for 20–25 minutes, sprinkling with cheese for the last 5 minutes of cooking.

4. To Microwave: Follow Steps 1 and 2 above. Arrange the peppers in an oiled microwave dish, sprinkle with cheese and microwave on High for 5–7 minutes.

MIKE'S PEPPERS AND EGGS

Serves 4

2 tablespoons vegetable oil
1 lb/500 g andouille, kielbasa or other smoked sausage, diced
$^1/_2$ red pepper (capsicum), seeded and diced
$^1/_2$ green pepper (capsicum), seeded and diced
$^1/_2$ yellow pepper (capsicum), seeded and diced
$^1/_2$ jalapeño or other hot green chilli, diced
$^1/_2$ onion, diced
6 eggs, lightly beaten
2 teaspoons Cajun Spice Mix (page 9)
1 teaspoon salt
$^1/_2$ cup/2 oz/60 g grated Cheddar cheese
Garnish:
1 tomato, diced
sour cream

1. In a large frying pan, heat the oil over medium high heat. Brown the sausage for 5–7 minutes, stirring well. Pour off all but about a tablespoon of the fat.

2. Add the peppers and onion and sauté over medium heat for 3–5 minutes.

3. Mix the eggs with the spice mix, salt and cheese and pour into the pan. If you prefer scrambled eggs, stir the mixture over medium low heat until done, 3–4 minutes. If you would rather make an omelette, let the eggs set over medium low heat for 3–4 minutes, then finish under a grill. Garnish with chopped tomato and sour cream.

HOT GREENS WITH POT LIKKER

Serves 6

Accompany these greens with Upcountry Cornbread (page 88) or Hellfire Biscuits (page 90) to dip into the savoury juice, or "pot likker".

3 lb/6 kg mixed greens: chard, mustard, kale, collard, etc.
2 cups/16 fl oz/500 ml water
2 tablespoons vegetable oil
8 oz/250 g spicy sausage (such as andouille) or
smoked ham, coarsely chopped
1 red onion, sliced
4 garlic cloves, chopped
2 tablespoons red wine vinegar
1 tablespoon Cajun Spice Mix (page 9)
$^1/_2$ teaspoon or more Tabasco or other hot pepper sauce
salt

1. Wash the greens thoroughly and separate any tough stems from the leaves. Chop stems and leaves separately. Bring the water to a boil in a large pot, add the stems and boil for 2–3 minutes. Put in the leaves, cover and steam for 3–5 minutes or until stems are tender and greens have wilted.

2. Heat the oil in a large frying pan and sauté the meat over medium high heat for 3–5 minutes. Pour off excess fat, leaving about $^1/_4$ cup/2 fl oz/60 ml in the pan. Add the onion and garlic and sauté for 3–5 minutes.

3. Add the contents of the pan to the greens and cook for 3–5 minutes over medium heat, stirring well. Add the vinegar, spice mix, Tabasco and salt and stir well. Taste for seasoning.

RED BEANS AND RICE

Serves 4–6

1 lb/500 g dried red or kidney beans
8 oz/250 g ham, cut into $^1/_2$ inch/1 cm dice
1 onion, chopped
1 green pepper (capsicum), seeded and chopped
$^1/_2$ cup/2 oz/60 g chopped celery
$^1/_4$ cup/1 oz/30 g chopped mild green chilli
4 garlic cloves, chopped
1 tablespoon Cajun Spice Mix (page 9)
1 teaspoon dried thyme or 2 teaspoons chopped fresh
$^1/_2$ teaspoon dried sage or 1 teaspoon chopped fresh
1 bay leaf
$^1/_4$ teaspoon or more Tabasco or other hot pepper sauce
1 tablespoon Worcestershire sauce
salt and pepper
cooked rice
chopped spring (green) onions and parsley for garnish

1. Put beans in a large saucepan, cover with water and soak overnight. Alternatively, to quick-soak the beans, bring to the boil, turn off heat, cover and soak for 1 hour before cooking. Discard the soaking water.

2. Cover the beans with fresh water and add all ingredients except salt, pepper, rice and garnish. Bring to the boil and simmer uncovered over low heat for 2–2$^1/_2$ hours or until the beans are tender, stirring occasionally and adding more water if they seem too dry. Season with salt and pepper. Ladle the beans over mounds of cooked rice in bowls, and garnish with spring onions and parsley.

DIRTY RICE

Serves 6

$^1/_3$ cup/2$^1/_2$ fl oz/80 ml vegetable oil
3 chicken or duck livers, chopped
1 cup/4 oz/125 g chopped spring (green) onions
1 tablespoon Cajun Spice Mix (page 9)
2 cups/14 oz/400 g uncooked rice
1 teaspoon salt
$^1/_4$ teaspoon black pepper
4$^1/_2$ cups/36 fl oz/1125 ml or more chicken stock or water

1. Heat the oil in a large pot with cover and sauté the livers and green onions over medium heat for 4–5 minutes. Sprinkle with spice mix and stir in rice, salt and pepper. Stir until rice is thoroughly coated with oil.

2. Add the stock and bring to the boil. Reduce heat to low, cover and cook for 25–30 minutes or until the rice is tender. Check after 20 minutes; if the rice seems too dry, add more stock or water.

GREEN RICE

Serves 6

$^{1}/_{3}$ cup/2$^{1}/_{2}$ fl oz/80 ml vegetable oil
1 cup/4 oz/125 g chopped spring (green) onions
$^{1}/_{2}$ cup/2 oz/60 g chopped parsley
1 cup/4 oz/125 g finely chopped green pepper (capsicum)
2 cups/14 oz/400 g uncooked rice
4$^{1}/_{2}$ cups/36 fl oz/1125 ml chicken stock or water
1 teaspoon salt
$^{1}/_{2}$ teaspoon black pepper

1. Heat the oil in a large saucepan with cover and sauté the chopped vegetables over medium heat for 3–5 minutes, stirring well. Add the rice and stir until well coated with oil.

2. Add the stock, salt and pepper and bring to the boil. Reduce heat to low, cover and cook for 25–30 minutes or until the rice is tender. Check after 20 minutes; if the rice seems too dry, add more chicken stock or water.

IRISH CHANNEL ROAST POTATOES

Serves 6

Serve with roast or grilled meats and poultry. Leftover potatoes are especially good for brunch when fried briefly in a little oil.

6 medium-size russet potatoes, cut into 2 inch/5 cm chunks
$^1/_4$ cup/2 fl oz/60 ml vegetable oil
1 tablespoon Cajun Spice Mix (page 9)
$1^1/_2$ teaspoons dried oregano or thyme
$1^1/_2$ teaspoons salt
$^1/_2$ teaspoon black pepper

1. Preheat oven to 375°F/190°C/Gas 5. Place the potatoes in a large bowl and toss with the oil. Mix in a small bowl the seasonings and sprinkle over the potatoes. Toss to coat thoroughly.

2. Transfer the potatoes to a well-oiled baking dish and bake, stirring occasionally, for 45 minutes–1 hour or until they are soft in the centre, crisp and brown on the outside. Serve at once.

YAM AND BOURBON SOUFFLÉ

Serves 6

A magnificent side dish with Barbecued Pork Roast (page 66) or Creole Pork Chops (page 67).

4 eggs, separated
2 cups/16 oz/500 g mashed cooked yams or
sweet potatoes (about 1¹/₂ lb/700 g raw)
¹/₂ cup/4 fl oz/125 ml cream
¹/₄ cup/2 fl oz/60 ml bourbon whisky
1¹/₂ tablespoons Southern Comfort or peach brandy
1¹/₂ tablespoons molasses
¹/₄ teaspoon grated nutmeg
¹/₄ teaspoon ground allspice
¹/₂ teaspoon salt

1. Blend the egg yolks, yams, cream, whisky, liqueur, molasses, spices and salt. Beat the egg whites to soft peaks.

2. Preheat oven to 350°F/180°C/Gas 4. Fold the egg whites into the yam mixture and transfer to an oiled 9 inch/23 cm soufflé dish. Bake for 35–40 minutes or until puffy and golden brown on top.

CREOLE VINAIGRETTE

Makes about 1¹/₄ cups/10 fl oz/300 ml

¹/₄ cup/2 fl oz/60 ml red wine vinegar
1 tablespoon Creole or other whole-grain mustard
2 garlic cloves, finely minced
1 teaspoon Cajun Spice Mix (page 9)
¹/₄ teaspoon cayenne
¹/₄ teaspoon Tabasco or other hot pepper sauce
1 teaspoon Worcestershire sauce
¹/₂ teaspoon or more salt
¹/₄ teaspoon black pepper
³/₄ cup/6 fl oz/175 ml olive or vegetable oil

1. Whisk together all ingredients except the oil in a small bowl. Gradually whisk in the oil.

2. Creole Vinaigrette will keep up to a week in a covered jar at cool room temperature.

SPINACH AND HOT PEPPER PECAN SALAD

Serves 4–6

4 cups fresh spinach (about 1 lb/450 g), cleaned and dried, torn for salad
$^{1}/_{2}$ red pepper (capsicum), seeded and cut into thin strips
$^{1}/_{4}$ cup/1 oz/30 g spring (green) onions
12 cherry tomatoes, halved
$^{1}/_{2}$ cup/4 fl oz/125 ml Creole Vinaigrette (page 78)
$^{1}/_{2}$ cup/3 oz/90 g Hot Pepper Pecans (page 11)
salt and pepper

1. Mix the spinach, red pepper, spring onions and cherry tomatoes in a large bowl.

2. Toss with Creole Vinaigrette and strew Hot Pepper Pecans on top of the salad. Taste for salt and pepper before serving.

CREOLE CHICKEN OR PRAWN SALAD

Serves 4

2 cups/8 oz/250 g diced cooked chicken or prawns
$^1/_4$ cup/1 oz/30 g finely chopped celery
$^1/_4$ cup/1 oz/30 g finely chopped onion
$^1/_4$ cup/1 oz/30 g finely chopped red or yellow pepper (capsicum)
1 teaspoon Cajun Spice Mix (page 9)
$^1/_4$ teaspoon Tabasco or other hot pepper sauce
1 teaspoon Worcestershire sauce
1 teaspoon dried tarragon or 2 teaspoons chopped fresh
1 teaspoon or more salt
$^1/_2$ cup/4 fl oz/125 ml mayonnaise
romaine (cos) lettuce leaves
Garnish:
halved cherry tomatoes
red pepper (capsicum) strips

Combine all but the last three ingredients. Spoon individual portions into lettuce leaves. Garnish with cherry tomatoes and pepper strips.

CAJUN RICE SALAD

Serves 6–8

4 cups/16 oz/500 g cooked long-grain rice, cooled
$^1/_2$ cup/2 oz/60 g chopped red pepper (capsicum)
$^1/_2$ cup/2 oz/60 g chopped green pepper (capsicum)
$^1/_4$ cup/1 oz/30 g chopped mild green chilli
$^1/_2$ cup/2 oz/60 g chopped red onion
$^1/_4$ cup/1 oz/30 g chopped celery
1 cup/8 fl oz/250 ml Creole Vinaigrette (page 78)
1 teaspoon or more salt
$^1/_4$ teaspoon or more black pepper
$^1/_2$ teaspoon or more Tabasco or other hot pepper sauce
$^1/_4$ cup/1 oz/30 g chopped spring (green) onions with tops
$^1/_4$ cup/$^1/_2$ oz/15 g chopped fresh parsley

Thoroughly combine all ingredients except the spring onions and parsley. Taste for salt, pepper and Tabasco. Sprinkle with chopped spring onions and parsley just before serving.

PICKLED PEPPER AND PRAWN SALAD

Serves 4–6 as an appetiser

1 cup/8 fl oz/250 ml white vinegar
2 tablespoons pickling spice
1 teaspoon red pepper flakes
2 teaspoons sugar
1 cup/8 fl oz/250 ml vegetable oil
$^{1}/_{2}$ red pepper (capsicum), seeded, quartered and thinly sliced
$^{1}/_{2}$ green pepper (capsicum), seeded, quartered and thinly sliced
$^{1}/_{2}$ yellow pepper (capsicum), seeded, quartered and thinly sliced
2 cups/8 oz/250 g cooked small prawns
$1^{1}/_{2}$ teaspoons dried dill or 1 tablespoon chopped fresh
1 teaspoon or more salt
$^{1}/_{4}$ teaspoon or more black pepper
$^{1}/_{4}$ teaspoon or more Tabasco or other hot pepper sauce
1 head butter or red lettuce
Garnish:
12 cherry tomatoes, halved
chopped fresh dill

1. Mix the vinegar, pickling spice, pepper flakes, sugar and oil in a non-aluminium saucepan and bring to the boil, then simmer over medium heat for 10 minutes. Strain over the peppers and prawns. Add the dill, salt, pepper and Tabasco and toss. Taste for seasoning.

2. Marinate the peppers and prawns in the refrigerator for at least 2 hours before serving. Remove from marinade with a slotted spoon. Arrange on lettuce leaves on individual plates or a platter. Garnish with cherry tomato halves. Spoon a little of the marinade on top and sprinkle with dill before serving.

PICKLED CORN AND OKRA SALAD

Serves 6

$^1/_2$ cup/4 fl oz/125 ml white vinegar
2 tablespoons sugar
2 tablespoons pickling spice
1 teaspoon red pepper flakes
$^1/_2$ cup/4 fl oz/125 ml vegetable oil
2 cups/8 oz/250 g fresh or defrosted frozen corn kernels
1 cup/4 oz/125 g chopped red pepper (capsicum)
1 cup/4 oz/125 g defrosted sliced frozen okra or parboiled fresh
(2–3 minutes)
1 cup/4 oz/125 g chopped spring (green) onions with tops
salt
Tabasco or other hot pepper sauce
1 head butter or red lettuce
Garnish:
12 cherry tomatoes, cut in half

1. Mix the vinegar, sugar, pickling spices, pepper flakes and oil in a nonaluminium saucepan and bring to the boil, then simmer over medium heat for 10 minutes. Strain over the corn, red pepper and okra. Marinate for at least 2 hours at room temperature, or overnight in the refrigerator. Stir in spring onions. Season with salt and Tabasco.

2. Arrange lettuce leaves on individual plates or a platter. Spoon the salad on top. Garnish with cherry tomato halves.

WILTED GREENS SALAD

Serves 6–8

2 lb/1 kg mixed greens such as kale, Savoy cabbage,
mustard, chard, turnip, beet, etc.
1 yellow pepper (capsicum), seeded and chopped
1 fennel bulb with top, chopped
1 cup/4 oz/125 g chopped spring (green) onions
8 oz/250 g spicy smoked sausage such as andouille, chopped
1 cup/8 fl oz/250 g Creole Vinaigrette (page 78)
salt, pepper and Tabasco or other hot pepper sauce

1. Mix the greens and chopped vegetables in a large salad bowl.
Sauté the sausage in a frying pan over medium high heat for 5–6
minutes. Add the sausage and the hot fat to the greens and toss well.

2. Pour the vinaigrette over the salad and toss to coat. Season with
salt, pepper and Tabasco.

DUCK CRACKLINS AND BITTER GREENS SALAD

Serves 6–8

1 cup/8 fl oz/250 ml vegetable oil
2 cups/8 oz/250 g leftover duck skin and meat from Spicy Roast
Duck (page 53), coarsely chopped
2 lb/1 kg mixed bitter greens such as mustard, kale, chard,
dandelions, radicchio, etc.
$^1/_2$ cup/2 oz/60 g chopped spring (green) onions
1 red pepper (capsicum), seeded and sliced
$^3/_4$ cup/6 fl oz/175 ml Creole Vinaigrette (page 78)
salt and pepper

1. Heat the oil in a frying pan over high heat and fry the duck skin
and meat in batches for 3–5 minutes, stirring and turning with a
slotted spoon until crisp. Remove cracklins as they cook with a
slotted spoon, and cool on paper towels.

2. Clean and dry the greens thoroughly, and discard any tough stems.
Tear the leaves roughly and place in a salad bowl. Mix the greens
with the onions and red pepper and toss with vinaigrette. Strew the
duck cracklins on top and serve.

PLAQUEMINE PARISH POTATO SALAD

Serves 6

8 medium-size waxy-skinned potatoes, unpeeled
$^1/_4$ cup/1 oz/30 g chopped red pepper (capsicum)
$^1/_4$ cup/1 oz/30 g chopped green pepper (capsicum)
$^1/_4$ cup/1 oz/30 g chopped celery
$^1/_2$ cup/2 oz/60 g chopped onion
1 teaspoon or more salt
$^1/_2$ teaspoon or more black pepper
1 cup/8 fl oz/250 ml Creole Vinaigrette (page 78)
$^1/_2$ teaspoon or more Tabasco or other hot pepper sauce
$^1/_2$ cup/2 oz/60 g chopped spring (green) onions with tops
$^1/_4$ cup/$^1/_2$ oz/15 g chopped parsley

1. Cook the whole potatoes in boiling salted water to cover until barely done, about 20–30 minutes depending on size. A sharp knife or skewer should meet some resistance when inserted. *Do not overcook the potatoes; they are better a little underdone than overcooked.* Cool until they can be handled but are still warm.

2. Cut the potatoes into $^1/_2$ inch/1 cm slices and place in a large bowl. Add the chopped peppers, celery and onion. Season with salt and pepper. While still warm, toss the mixture with the vinaigrette and Tabasco. Marinate for at least 1 hour at room temperature, turning occasionally. Before serving toss with the spring onions and parsley, and taste for salt, pepper and Tabasco.

GREEN CHILLI CORNBREAD

Serves 6–8

1 cup/5$^{1}/_{2}$ oz/150 g yellow cornmeal
$^{1}/_{2}$ cup/2 oz/60 g plain flour
1 tablespoon baking powder
$^{1}/_{2}$ teaspoon salt
2 teaspoons Cajun Spice Mix (page 9)
$^{1}/_{4}$ cup/1 oz/30 g finely chopped mild green chilli
1$^{1}/_{2}$ tablespoons or more finely chopped hot green chilli
$^{1}/_{4}$ cup/1 oz/30 g finely chopped spring (green) onions with tops
1 egg
$^{3}/_{4}$ cup/6 fl oz/175 ml milk
3 tablespoons corn oil

1. Preheat oven to 425°F/220°C/Gas 7. Mix the dry ingredients with the chillies and onion. Combine the liquid ingredients and stir into the dry ingredients to make a thick batter.

2. Generously oil a 9 inch/22.5 cm square baking pan or a deep-dish pie plate. Spoon the batter into the pan and bake for about 20 minutes or until firm to the touch at the centre. Serve hot.

UPCOUNTRY CORNBREAD

Serves 6–8

1 cup/5¹/₂ oz/150 g yellow cornmeal
¹/₂ cup/2 oz/60 g plain flour
1 tablespoon baking powder
¹/₂ teaspoon salt
1 egg, lightly beaten
³/₄ cup/6 fl oz/175 ml milk
3 tablespoons vegetable oil
1 cup/4 oz/125 g cooked fresh or frozen corn
¹/₄ cup/1 oz/30 g chopped red pepper (capsicum)
¹/₄ cup/1 oz/30 g chopped spring (green) onions with tops

1. Preheat oven to 425°F/220°C/Gas 7. Mix the dry ingredients. Combine the liquid ingredients with the corn, and stir into the dry ingredients to make a thick batter.

2. Generously oil a 9 inch/22.5 cm square baking pan or a deep-dish pie plate. Spoon the batter into the pan and bake for about 20 minutes or until firm to the touch at the centre. Serve hot.

SWEET POTATO PECAN PUFFS

Serves 6–8

Marvellous with fresh peach jam for breakfast or with Barbecued Pork Roast (page 66) and Yam Bourbon Soufflé (page 77).

2 cups/8 oz/250 g plain flour
$2^1/_2$ teaspoons baking powder
$^1/_2$ teaspoon bicarbonate of soda
$^1/_2$ teaspoon salt
$^1/_4$ cup/2 fl oz/60 ml vegetable oil
$^3/_4$ cup/6 fl oz/175 ml buttermilk or $^3/_4$ cup/6 fl oz/175 ml milk plus
1 teaspoon lemon juice
1 cup/8 oz/250 g mashed cooked sweet potatoes or
yams (about $^3/_4$ lb/350 g raw)
$^1/_2$ teaspoon ground ginger
$^1/_4$ teaspoon ground allspice
$^1/_4$ cup/1 oz/30 g chopped pecans
1 tablespoon molasses
1 tablespoon sugar

1. Preheat oven to 450°F/230°C/Gas 8. Thoroughly mix the flour, baking powder, bicarbonate of soda and salt. Blend the remaining ingredients in another bowl and add to the flour mixture all at once. Stir only until evenly combined.

2. By tablespoons, spoon the dough onto a lightly oiled baking pan or biscuit tray. Uncooked puffs should be about 2 inches/5 cm in diameter, spaced at least 1 inch/2.5 cm apart.

3. Bake for about 15 minutes or until puffed and lightly browned.

HELLFIRE BISCUITS

Serves 6–8

2 cups/8 oz/250 g plain flour
1 tablespoon finely chopped hot or mild green chilli
1 tablespoon finely chopped red pepper (capsicum)
2 tablespoons finely chopped spring (green) onions
1$^{1}/_{2}$ teaspoons Cajun Spice Mix (page 9)
1 tablespoon baking powder
$^{1}/_{2}$ teaspoon salt
$^{1}/_{4}$ cup/2 fl oz/60 ml vegetable oil
$^{3}/_{4}$ cup/6 fl oz/175 ml milk

1. Preheat oven to 450°F/230°C/Gas 8. Stir the flour with the peppers, onion and remaining dry ingredients to distribute everything evenly. Stir in liquids to make a dough.

2. Spoon the dough by tablespoons onto a lightly oiled baking pan or biscuit tray, shaping the biscuits with your fingers into 2 inch/7.5 cm rounds. Bake for about 20 minutes or until they begin to brown on top. Serve immediately.

DIXIE BEER HUSHPUPPIES

Serves 6–8

Hushpuppies are savoury bits of fried polenta (cornmeal) and spices that were used to hush up the puppies on camping and hunting trips. They are especially good with fish (Blackened Fish Fillets, page 41, or Grilled Sea Bass Diable, page 42) and a spicy sauce such as Sauce Piquante (page 51) or Tomato Lime Chilli Sauce (page 15).

$1^1/_2$ cups/8 oz/250 g polenta (cornmeal)
$^1/_2$ cup/2 oz/60 g plain flour
1 tablespoon Cajun Spice Mix (page 9)
$^1/_4$ teaspoon cayenne
1 teaspoon dried thyme
2 teaspoons baking powder
1 $^1/_2$ teaspoons salt
2 tablespoons finely chopped spring (green) onion tops
1 egg
$^3/_4$ cup/6 fl oz/175 ml light lager beer
vegetable oil for deep frying

1. Blend the dry ingredients and onion. Beat the egg with the beer and add gradually to the dry mixture, stirring to make a thick batter. Let stand for 10–15 minutes before using.

2. Heat 2–3 inches/5–7.5 cm of oil in a heavy frying pan to 350°F/180°C. Test with a bit of batter; it should sizzle in the hot oil. Drop in the batter by tablespoonfuls, being careful not to crowd the pan. Fry for 1–2 minutes per side or until deep golden brown. Remove hushpuppies as they cook and drain on paper towels.

COUSH-COUSH

Serves 6–8

Traditionally served with fried sausage patties for breakfast, with cane or maple syrup.

1 cup/5$^{1}/_{2}$ oz/150 g polenta (cornmeal)
1 tablespoon flour
1 teaspoon baking powder
$^{1}/_{4}$ teaspoon salt
1$^{1}/_{4}$ cups/10 fl oz/300 ml water
1$^{1}/_{2}$ tablespoons vegetable oil
3$^{1}/_{2}$ tablespoons butter
2 cups/16 fl oz/500 ml milk
1 cup/8 fl oz/250 ml cream
2 tablespoons molasses
cane or maple syrup

1. Mix the polenta, flour, baking powder, salt and water to make a thick batter. Heat the oil and 2$^{1}/_{2}$ tablespoons of the butter in a nonstick frying pan over medium high heat and pour in the polenta batter. Cook over medium heat for 7–10 minutes or until a golden brown crust forms on the bottom.

2. Turn and stir the batter, breaking up the crust and mixing it in. Stir in 1 tablespoon butter and 1 cup/8 fl oz/250 ml milk, cover and cook over medium heat for 10 minutes, stirring occasionally. Add the remaining milk with the cream and molasses, stirring well. Cook for a few more minutes, covered, to heat through.

3. Serve from the pan or invert onto a platter.

SPOONBREAD OR CORN PUDDING

Serves 6

This is more like a pudding or soft soufflé than a bread. It's a wonderful accompaniment to Baked Chicken Creole (page 49) or Barbecued Pork Roast (page 66), or try it for lunch or a light dinner with Grillades (page 57) and Wilted Greens Salad (page 84).

2^1/$_2$ cups/20 fl oz/600 ml milk
2 cups/8 oz/250 g fresh or frozen sweetcorn kernels
^{1}/$_2$ cup/2^1/$_2$ oz/75 g polenta (cornmeal)
2 tablespoons salted butter
^{1}/$_2$ teaspoon salt
^{1}/$_4$ teaspoon black pepper
2 tablespoons Cajun Spice Mix (page 9)
^{1}/$_2$ teaspoon dried thyme or 1 teaspoon chopped fresh
2 tablespoons chopped spring (green) onions with tops
3 eggs, separated

1. Preheat oven to 350°F/180°C/Gas 4. Bring milk to the boil. Add the corn and polenta and simmer, stirring, until thick, about 5 minutes. Remove from heat and stir in the butter, seasonings and onion.

2. Beat the egg yolks with a spoonful of the warm corn mixture, then add to remaining mixture. Beat the egg whites until stiff and gently fold into the corn mixture.

3. Turn the spoonbread batter into a buttered 9 inch/23 cm soufflé dish. Bake about 45 minutes until browned on top and set in the middle.

PAIN PERDU

Serves 4

$^1/_2$ cup/4 fl oz/125 ml cream or half and half
1 cup/8 fl oz/250 ml milk
2 tablespoons Southern Comfort or peach brandy
4 eggs, lightly beaten
$^1/_4$ cup/2 oz/60 g sugar
1/2 teaspoon vanilla essence
2 tablespoons or more vegetable oil
8 slices French bread, $^1/_2$–$^3/_4$ inch/1–1.5 cm thick
icing sugar and cinnamon
Spiced Peach Syrup (page 95) or cane syrup

1. Mix the cream, milk, liqueur, eggs, sugar and vanilla in a shallow bowl. Heat the oil in a large frying pan over medium high heat.

2. Dip the bread slices into the milk mixture, letting them soak for 1–2 minutes. Fry the bread 2–3 minutes on a side or until golden brown, adding more oil if necessary.

3. Sprinkle the Pain Perdu with icing sugar and a little cinnamon before serving for brunch or dessert with Spiced Peach Syrup or cane syrup.

SPICED PEACH SYRUP

Makes about 1¹/₂ cups/12 fl oz/350 ml

2 cups/16 fl oz/500 ml liquid from cooked peaches or other fruit
¹/₄ cup/2 fl oz/60 ml Southern Comfort or peach brandy
¹/₄ cup/2 fl oz/60 ml or more corn syrup
1 cinnamon stick
4 whole cloves
4 whole allspice
1 cup chopped cooked peaches (optional)

1. Combine the peach liquid, liqueur, corn syrup and spices in a saucepan and bring to the boil. Reduce heat and simmer for 30 minutes or until the liquid is reduced to a syrup. Taste for sweetness and add more corn syrup if desired.

2. Let the syrup cool. Remove spices, and add 1 cup coarsely chopped cooked peaches if desired. Serve syrup warm, or store covered in the refrigerator for up to a week.

3. If using canned peaches in syrup: Cook strained syrup with liqueur and spices (omit corn syrup) until reduced by about half.

LOBSTER OR PRAWN PIE

Serves 4–6

$^1/_2$ cup/4 fl oz/125 ml vegetable oil
$^2/_3$ cup/3 oz/85 g plain flour
1 onion, chopped
$^1/_2$ green pepper (capsicum), seeded and chopped
$^1/_2$ red pepper (capsicum), seeded and chopped
$^1/_4$ cup/1 oz/30 g chopped mild green chilli
$^1/_2$ cup/2 oz/60 g chopped celery
$1^1/_2$ cups/12 fl oz/350 ml fish or chicken stock
$^1/_4$ cup/2 fl oz/60 ml cream
$^1/_4$ cup/2 fl oz/60 ml dry sherry
1 tablespoon tomato paste (concentrate)
1 teaspoon dried basil or 2 teaspoons chopped fresh
1 teaspoon dried marjoram or 2 teaspoons chopped fresh
$^1/_4$ teaspoon cayenne
2 tablespoons Cajun Spice Mix (page 9)
1 teaspoon salt
$^1/_4$ teaspoon black pepper
1 lb/500 g shelled lobster or small prawns
$^1/_2$ cup/2 oz/60 g chopped spring (green) onions with tops
2 recipes Nutty Pie Crust (page 108)—substitute $1^1/_2$ teaspoons Cajun
Spice Mix for $^1/_4$ cup/1 oz/30 g chopped nuts in each recipe

1. Make a peanut butter roux (see "Making a Roux", page 8) using the oil and flour, or reheat 1 cup/8 oz/250 g prepared roux in a heavy frying pan. Add vegetables and cook over medium heat for 3–4 minutes.

2. Stir in the stock, cream, sherry, tomato paste, herbs, spices, salt and pepper and cook for 8–10 minutes. Add seafood, and simmer 3–5 minutes. Stir in the spring onions and taste for seasoning. Cool, cover and refrigerate for at least 3 hours or overnight.

3. Preheat oven to 425°F/220°C/Gas 7. Roll out 1 recipe of the pie crust $^1/_4$ inch/5 mm thick, following the directions on page 108, and line a 9 inch/22.5 cm deep-dish pie plate or individual ramekins with the crust. Bake 7–8 minutes, checking after 4 minutes. Pressing down any bubbles.

4. Cool the crust and spoon in the lobster or prawn mixture. Cover with another recipe of pie crust completely or in a lattice pattern. Slash top if covering pie completely. Bake for 45 minutes. Serve hot.

NATCHITOCHES MEAT PIE

Makes 6

Serve hot or cold with Sauce Piquante (page 51) as an appetiser, snack or light lunch.

1 tablespoon vegetable oil
8 oz/250 g lean ground beef
8 oz/250 g ground pork
$^{1}/_{4}$ cup/1 oz/30 g chopped onion
$^{1}/_{4}$ cup/1 oz/30 g chopped mild green chilli
$^{3}/_{4}$ cup/6 oz/175 g chopped cooked potato
$1^{1}/_{2}$ teaspoons Cajun Spice Mix (page 9)
1 teaspoon powdered sage
$^{1}/_{4}$ teaspoon cayenne
$^{1}/_{2}$ teaspoon salt
$^{1}/_{4}$ teaspoon black pepper
Pastry:
$1^{1}/_{2}$ cups/6 oz/175 g plain flour
$^{1}/_{2}$ teaspoon Cajun Spice Mix
1 teaspoon milk
$^{1}/_{2}$ cup/4 fl oz/125 ml vegetable oil
$^{1}/_{4}$ cup/2 fl oz/60 ml boiling water

1. Heat the oil in a frying pan and brown the meats over medium high heat, stirring frequently, for 2–3 minutes. Add the onion and chilli and sauté for 2–3 minutes. Drain off fat. Combine the meat mixture with the remaining filling ingredients in a large bowl.

2. Preheat oven to 425°F/220°C/Gas 7. Mix all the pastry ingredients to make a dough. Divide the dough into sixths and roll out between sheets of greaseproof paper into rounds about $^{1}/_{4}$ inch/5 mm thick. Arrange on a lightly greased baking tray.

3. Place a sixth of the filling on one side of a pastry round, fold over and press the edges together with the back of a fork. Repeat with the remaining pastry rounds. Prick each turnover with a fork once or twice, and bake for 20 minutes or until browned.

MEGHAN'S AMBROSIA CAKE

Serves 8–10

³/₄ cup/6 fl oz/175 ml mashed banana (1 large banana)
1¹/₄ cups/8 oz/230 g sugar
¹/₂ cup/4 fl oz/125 ml corn oil
2 eggs, lightly beaten
1¹/₂ tablespoons grated orange rind
2¹/₃ cups/9¹/₂ oz/270 g plain flour
³/₄ teaspoon bicarbonate of soda
1 teaspoon baking powder
¹/₄ teaspoon salt
³/₄ cup/6 fl oz/175 ml orange juice
2 cups/16 fl oz/500 ml whipping (thick) cream
1 cup/8 oz/250 g canned crushed pineapple
2 tablespoons Southern Comfort or peach brandy
1 cup/4 oz/125 g desiccated coconut

1. Cream together the banana, sugar, corn oil, eggs and orange rind. Add flour, bicarbonate of soda, baking powder, salt and orange juice and mix well.

2. Preheat oven to 350°F/180°C/Gas 4. Lightly butter and flour two 9 inch/22.5 cm round layer cake tins or a 13 x 9 x 2 inch/32.5 x 22.5 x 5 cm slab cake tin. Pour in the batter and bake until the top springs back when touched in the centre, about 30 minutes for layers or 40 minutes for a slab cake. Cool in the tin for about 10 minutes, then turn out on a rack to cool completely.

3. For a layer cake, whip half of the cream and fold in all the pineapple. Spread between the layers. Whip the other cup of cream with the liqueur and spread over the top and sides. Sprinkle the top with coconut. For a slab cake, whip all the cream, fold in the pineapple and liqueur, spread over the top and sides and top with coconut. Chill for about an hour before serving.

MAHOGANY CAKE WITH PECAN FUDGE FROSTING

Serves 8

³/₄ cup/6 oz/170 g sweetened cocoa powder
1 cup/8 oz/250 g packed brown sugar
¹/₂ cup/4 fl oz/125 ml molasses
1 cup/8 fl oz/250 ml boiling water
³/₄ cup/6 fl oz/175 ml corn oil
3 eggs
2 tablespoons dark rum
2¹/₂ cups/12 oz/350 g plain flour
2 teaspoons bicarbonate of soda
¹/₂ teaspoon salt
1 teaspoon cinnamon
Frosting:
3 oz/85 g unsweetened chocolate
3 tablespoons butter
2 tablespoons molasses
5 tablespoons cream
3 cups/8 oz/250 g icing sugar
pecan halves or finely chopped pecans for garnish

1. Preheat oven to 350°F/180°C/Gas 4. Mix the cocoa, brown sugar, molasses and boiling water; cool. Beat in the oil, eggs, rum, flour, bicarbonate of soda, salt and cinnamon.

2. Butter and flour an 8 or 9 inch/20 or 22.5 cm round cake tin or a 13 x 9 x 2 inch/32.5 x 22.5 x 5 cm slab cake tin. Pour batter into cake tins and bake about 25 minutes for layers, 40 minutes for a slab cake, until cake springs back lightly when pressed in the centre.

3. For the frosting, melt chocolate and butter in a double saucepan or in the microwave (about 1¹/₂ minutes on High). Add the molasses and beat in the cream and sugar, alternating 1 tablespoon cream with ¹/₂ cup/¹/₃ oz/40 g icing sugar. Spread on cooled cake. Decorate with pecan halves or finely chopped pecans.

PEACH MOLASSES UPSIDE DOWN CAKE

Serves 8–10

Serve this as is or topped with Mango Peach Cream (page 102).

$^1/_4$ cup/2 oz/60 g salted butter
$^1/_2$ cup/4 oz/125 g packed brown sugar
1 cup/8 oz/250 g sliced cooked or canned peaches
2 cups/8 oz/250 g plain flour
2 teaspoons baking powder
$^1/_2$ teaspoon bicarbonate of soda
$^3/_4$ cup/5 oz/150 g sugar
$^1/_4$ cup/2 fl oz/60 ml molasses
$^3/_4$ cup/6 fl oz/175 ml orange juice
$^1/_3$ cup/2$^1/_2$ fl oz/80 ml vegetable oil or melted butter
2 eggs

1. Preheat oven to 350°F/180°C/Gas 4. Melt $^1/_4$ cup/2 oz/60 g butter in a 9 inch/22.5 cm square cake tin. Mix in the brown sugar and top with peaches.

2. Beat the remaining ingredients together and spread over the fruit. Bake for about 30 minutes or until a knife inserted in the centre comes out clean.

BANANA PECAN COFFEE CAKE WITH PRALINE TOPPING

Serves 8

2 cups/16 oz/500 g mashed bananas (3 large bananas)
3^1/$_2$ cups/14 oz/400 g flour
4 teaspoons baking powder
^{2}/$_3$ cup/5 oz/150 ml vegetable oil
1^1/$_3$ cups/9 oz/250 g sugar
2 eggs
^{2}/$_3$ cup/3 oz/85 g chopped pecans
Praline Topping:
^{1}/$_4$ cup/2 oz/60 g butter
1 cup/8 oz/250 g packed brown sugar
^{1}/$_4$ cup/1 oz/30 g plain flour
^{1}/$_2$ teaspoon grated nutmeg
1 cup/4 oz/125 g pecan halves

1. Preheat oven to 350°F/180°C/Gas 4. Thoroughly mix all the cake ingredients and spread in an oiled 13 x 9 x 2 inch/32.5 x 22.5 x 5 cm cake tin.

2. For the topping, melt the butter in a saucepan over medium heat. Stir in the sugar, flour, nutmeg and pecans. Smooth the praline mixture over the batter. Decorate with pecan halves. Bake for 1 hour or until a tester inserted in the centre comes out clean. Cool before serving.

MANGO PEACH CREAM

Makes 3¹/₂ cups/32 fl oz/875 ml

2 ripe mangoes (if not available, substitute peaches)
2 ripe peaches or nectarines
1 cup/8 fl oz/250 ml whipping (thick) cream
2 tablespoons or more sugar
2 tablespoons Southern Comfort or peach brandy
fresh fruit or berries for garnish (optional)

1. Peel and slice the fruit. Simmer in water to cover until tender, about 5 minutes. Drain and coarsely purée the fruit (reserve the cooking liquid for Spiced Peach Syrup, page 95, if desired). There should be about 2 cups/16 fl oz/500 ml of purée.

2. Whip the cream with the sugar and liqueur, adding more sugar if the fruit is tart. Fold the whipped cream into the fruit purée. Spoon into individual dishes or a glass bowl and chill before serving. Garnish with fruit or berries to serve as dessert, or serve as a sauce over Spiced Peach Crêpes (page 103) or Pain Perdu (page 94).

SPICED PEACH CRÊPES

Serves 4–6

1 cup/4 oz/125 g plain flour
1 tablespoon sugar
3 eggs
2 tablespoons butter, melted
¹/₂ teaspoon vanilla essence
2 tablespoons Southern Comfort
1¹/₂ cups/12 fl oz/350 ml milk
butter for cooking crêpes
2 cups/16 oz/500 g cooked sliced fresh or canned peaches
1 recipe Spiced Peach Syrup (page 95)
1 recipe Mango Peach Cream (page 102), optional

1. Mix the flour and sugar and beat in the eggs one at a time. Stir in the melted butter, vanilla, liqueur and milk.

2. Melt 1 tablespoon butter in a heavy 6–9 inch/15–22.5 cm saucepan over medium high heat. When the saucepan is well heated, spoon in just enough batter to thinly cover the bottom, tilting and swirling the pan to distribute the batter evenly.

3. When the edges of the crêpe turn light brown, loosen it with a spatula and turn. Cook for another minute and remove from the saucepan. Stack the crêpes between sheets of greaseproof paper as they are cooked. At this point you can serve them or refrigerate for later use.

4. Place a line of peaches down the centre of each crêpe, moisten with a little Spiced Peach Syrup, and roll up neatly. Spoon more syrup over the crêpes and top with Mango Peach Cream, if desired.

CREOLE RICE PUDDING

Serves 6–8

This flavourful Creole pudding can be served on its own, with Whisky Sauce (page 105) or Mango Peach Cream (page 102), or topped with meringue.

$1^{1}/_{2}$ cups/12 fl oz/350 ml water
$^{1}/_{2}$ cup/$3^{1}/_{2}$ oz/100 g long-grain rice
2 cups/16 fl oz/500 ml milk
1 cup/8 fl oz/250 ml cream
2 tablespoons Southern Comfort or peach brandy
1 teaspoon vanilla essence
1 cup/$6^{1}/_{2}$ oz/190 g sugar
$^{1}/_{2}$ cup/2 oz/60 g chopped dried fruit, such as apricots or peaches, or whole raisins
3 eggs, whole or separated if you wish to make optional meringue
pinch of salt for meringue (optional)

1. Bring the water and rice to the boil in a saucepan, cover and simmer for about 20 minutes or until the water is absorbed and rice is tender. Cool.

2. Preheat oven to 300°F/150°C/Gas 2. Mix the rice with the remaining ingredients, including the lightly beaten whole eggs or, if you choose to make meringue, the yolks only. Bake uncovered for about 1 hour or until firm. Serve warm or refrigerate for later use.

3. To make meringue, preheat oven to 400°F/200°C/Gas 6. Beat egg whites with pinch of salt until they form soft peaks. Cover the cooked pudding with the meringue and bake until lightly browned, about 10 minutes. Serve immediately.

WHISKY SAUCE

Makes 1¹/₄ cups/10 fl oz/300 ml

Whisky Sauce is traditionally served on Bread Pudding (page 106), but it is also delicious on Creole Rice Pudding (page 104) or Persimmon Pudding (page 107).

1 cup/8 fl oz/250 ml cream
¹/₄ cup/2 fl oz/60 ml bourbon whisky
1 tablespoon cornflour
¹/₂ teaspoon vanilla essence
2 tablespoons sugar
1 egg
¹/₄ teaspoon grated nutmeg
¹/₈ teaspoon ground allspice

1. In a small saucepan, heat the cream over medium high heat until bubbles start to form around the edge. Stir together the whisky and cornflour and add to the cream, whisking vigorously. Lower heat and cook until the cream begins to thicken, 1–2 minutes, whisking occasionally. Stir in the vanilla and sugar.

2. Break the egg in a small bowl and whisk in 1 tablespoon of the hot cream. Repeat with 2–3 more tablespoons of cream, one at a time, until the egg mixture is warmed through. Remove the cream from the heat and whisk in the egg mixture and spices to make a smooth sauce. Return to low heat and cook for 1–2 minutes more, whisking often, until sauce reaches the consistency of thick cream. Serve warm or cool.

BREAD PUDDING

Serves 8–10

Serve with Whisky Sauce (page 105) or Mango Peach Cream (page 102).

4 eggs, lightly beaten
1 cup/8 oz/250 g firmly packed brown sugar
3 cups/24 fl oz/750 ml light cream
1 teaspoon cinnamon
$^1/_2$ teaspoon grated nutmeg
$^1/_4$ teaspoon ground cloves
2 cups/8 oz/250 g chopped apples or other fruit, or whole raisins
10 cups/20 oz/600 g French bread torn into small pieces

1. Mix the eggs, sugar, cream and spices, and pour over the apples and bread in a large bowl. Stir well. Let the mixture soak for about 30 minutes, stirring occasionally.

2. Preheat oven to 300°F/150°C/Gas 2. Lightly butter a 9 inch/22.5 cm square baking dish. Pour in the pudding mixture and bake until firm and beginning to brown, about 1 hour. Cool before serving.

PERSIMMON PUDDING

Serves 6–8

Serve with whipped cream or Whisky Sauce (page 105).

2 cups/13 oz/380 g sugar
2 cups/16 fl oz/500 ml persimmon pulp
2 eggs, beaten
1 teaspoon bicarbonate of soda
1$^1/_2$ cups/12 fl oz/350 ml buttermilk
1$^1/_2$ cups/6 oz/175 g plain flour
$^1/_8$ teaspoon salt
2 teaspoons baking powder
1 tablespoon vanilla essence
$^1/_4$ cup/2 oz/60 g salted butter, melted
$^1/_4$ cup/2 fl oz/60 ml cream

Preheat oven to 350°F/180°C/Gas 4. Thoroughly mix all ingredients
and spread in a buttered 9$^1/_2$ inch/23 cm soufflé dish or 13 x 9 x 2
inch/32.5 x 22.5 x 5 cm pan. Bake for 45 minutes or until a knife
inserted halfway between the edge and the centre comes out clean
(the pudding doesn't have to be completely firm at the centre; it will
continue to cook, and deflate somewhat, as it cools).

NUTTY PIE CRUST

Makes one 9 inch/22.5 cm crust

1 tablespoon butter
1¹/₂ cups/6 oz/175 g plain flour
¹/₄ cup/1 oz/30 g finely chopped pecans or other nuts
¹/₂ teaspoon salt
1 teaspoon milk
¹/₂ cup/4 fl oz/125 ml vegetable oil
¹/₄ cup/2 fl oz/60 ml boiling water

1. Lightly butter a 9 inch/22.5 cm deep-dish pie plate. Preheat oven to 425°F/220°C/Gas 7. Blend all ingredients thoroughly to form a dough.

2. Roll the dough out between two sheets of greaseproof paper to a thickness of about ¹/₄ inch/5 mm. Peel off the top layer of paper and invert the dough over the pie plate. Peel off the other piece of paper and press the dough into the pan, crimping the edges. Prick the base of the crust all over with a fork. Bake for about 7 minutes if you are going to add a filling that will be baked longer; bake 15 minutes for a fully baked pie shell. While the crust is baking, press down any bubbles that might arise. Cool before filling.

KATHY'S PECAN PIE

Serves 8

$^1/_4$ cup/2 oz/60 g salted butter, melted
1 cup/8 oz/250 g packed brown sugar
1 cup/8 fl oz/250 ml dark corn syrup
$^1/_2$ teaspoon salt
2 tablespoons bourbon whisky or 1 teaspoon vanilla essence
4 eggs
1$^1/_2$ cups/6 oz/175 g broken pecans
1 partially baked (7 minutes) Nutty Pie Crust (page 108) or
other 9 inch/22.5 cm pie crust

1. Stir together the butter, brown sugar, corn syrup, salt and whisky or vanilla in a large bowl. Beat in the eggs one at a time. Stir in the pecans.

2. Preheat oven to 375°F/190°C/Gas 5. Pour the mixture into the partially baked pie shell and bake for 45–50 minutes or until firm at the centre. Cool before serving.

CHOCOLATE PECAN PIE

Serves 8

2 oz/60 g unsweetened chocolate
3 tablespoons salted butter
1 cup/8 oz/250 g packed dark brown sugar
$^1/_2$ cup/4 fl oz/125 ml molasses
2 tablespoons bourbon whisky
4 eggs
2 cups/8 oz/250 g broken pecans
1 partially baked (7 minutes) Nutty Pie Crust (page 108) or
other 9 inch/22.5 cm pie crust

1. Melt the chocolate and butter in a double saucepan or in the microwave on High for about $1^1/_2$ minutes. In a large bowl, blend the chocolate mixture, brown sugar, molasses and whisky. Beat in eggs one at a time. Stir in the pecans.

2. Preheat oven to 375°F/190°C/Gas 5. Pour the mixture into the partially baked pie shell and bake for 45–50 minutes or until firm at the centre. Cool before serving.

CHOCOLATE WHISKY CREAM PIE

Serves 8

2 oz/60 g sweet chocolate
3 cups/24 fl oz/750 ml milk
¹/₂ cup/4 fl oz/125 ml molasses
2 tablespoons bourbon whisky
3 tablespoons cornflour
¹/₈ teaspoon bicarbonate of soda
2 eggs
1 tablespoon salted butter, melted
1 fully baked (15 minutes) Nutty Pie Crust (page 108) or
other 9 inch/22.5 cm pie crust
1 cup/8 fl oz/250 ml whipping (thick) cream
1 tablespoon sweetened cocoa powder

1. Mix the chocolate, milk, molasses, 1 tablespoon bourbon, cornflour and bicarbonate of soda in a saucepan and heat gently, stirring frequently. Beat the eggs in a bowl and add the warm mixture a tablespoon at a time until the eggs are warmed through. Add the egg mixture to the pan and continue to cook over low heat, stirring, until the mixture thickens, about 10 minutes. Remove from heat and stir in the remaining bourbon and the melted butter. Cool.

2. Pour the cooled mixture into the baked pie shell. Whip the cream with the cocoa and spread over the filling. Chill for at least an hour before serving.

SWEET POTATO PIE

Serves 8

2 cups/16 oz/500 g puréed, cooked sweet potatoes or
yams (about 1$^1/_2$ lb/1 kg raw)
1$^1/_2$ cups/12 fl oz/350 ml evaporated milk
3 eggs
$^3/_4$ cup/5 oz/140 g sugar
$^1/_4$ teaspoon salt
$^1/_2$ teaspoon cinnamon
$^1/_2$ teaspoon grated nutmeg
$^1/_2$ teaspoon ground ginger
1 partially baked (7 minutes) Nutty Pie Crust (page 108) or
other 9 inch/22.5 cm pie crust, with $^1/_2$ teaspoon cinnamon added to recipe
1 cup/8 fl oz/250 ml whipping (thick) cream, whipped with
1 tablespoon Southern Comfort or
peach brandy and 1 tablespoon sugar (optional)

Preheat oven to 450°F/230°C/Gas 8. Combine all ingredients except
pie shell and whipped cream. Pour filling into partially baked pie
shell. Bake for 10 minutes. Reduce heat to 350°F/180°C/Gas 4 and
bake another 40 minutes or until set in the middle. Cool and serve as
is or with optional whipped cream.

GLOSSARY

Andouille: A smoked sausage, popular in Louisiana, made from chunks of pork, garlic and spices. It adds spice and flavour to soups, stews and gumbos. Substitute kielbasa or smoked sausage and add a bit more garlic and a pinch or two of cayene.

Allspice: (Jamaican pepper) These small dried berries are the size of a pea and have a taste which resembles a peppery compound of cloves, cinnamon and nutmeg. They are used whole or ground and it is preferable to buy allspice whole and grind as needed.

Beet: (silverbeet, seakale, spinach, Swiss chard) A vegetable with dark green, glossy leaves and white stems. It is an excellent source of vitamins A and C, and iron, but has a high sodium content.

Bisque: A thick soup usually made from seafood, such as crab, prawns or lobster.

Burgoo: A savoury game stew of meat, poultry, peppers (capsicums), corn, okra and what you will; popular throughout the American South at fishing camps and on hunting trips.

Buttermilk: This is the liquid remaining after fresh cream has been churned to make butter. Semi-skinned milk can be used as a substitute.

Chard: See beet.

Collard: A variety of kale: cabbage can be used as a substitute.

Coriander: Mexican or Chinese parsley (sometimes called cilantro). The flavour of the coriander leaf does not resemble that of its seed. Parsley or basil are fairly adequate substitutes.

Corn syrup: This golden syrup is made from cornstarch and water. Glucose syrup or liquid honey are adequate alternatives.

Cornmeal (polenta)**:** Corn (maize) is ground to form this fine yellow powder. It originated in Central America and was the staple food of the Incas. Its popularity spread to North America and then Europe where it is more familiar to us as the Italian dish polenta.

Dandelion greens: The deeply notched leaves at the base of the common dandelion are a delicious addition to a green salad. If not available, endive is a good alternative.

Dill seed: This mid-brown, oval seed of the dill plant has a warm, pungent, slightly sharp aroma and a taste that resembles caraway.

Etouffée: Literally "smothered", this technique uses large amounts of onions, peppers (capsicums) and butter to "smother" seafoods such as lobster, prawns and other foods.

Filé powder (gumbo filé)**:** Dried ground sassafras bark and thyme, used to thicken and flavour gumbos. Always add after the saucepan is removed from the heat; otherwise the filé will clot and become ropy.

Fennel seed: Like the bulb, fennel's greenish-yellow seeds have a slight aniseed flavour.

Gumbo: Popular spicy soup/stew found all over Louisiana and made from a variety of ingredients. Usually begins with a dark roux, often combines fish, seafood, poultry and/or meat, and is thickened with okra or filé powder.

Heavy cream: Double cream.

Hushpuppies: One of many cornmeal breads found throughout the region. Cornmeal is mixed with spices, beer, buttermilk or milk, and egg, and deep-fried. Popular on hunting trips, where they were used to hush the hunting dogs around the campfire.

Jalapeño (chilli, cuaresmeno, lenten chilli): A bright green to dark green chilli, sometimes greenish black in colour. About two inches long by three–quarters of an inch wide, it is extremely hot.

Jambalaya: A rice-based dish of Spanish origin, usually incorporating ham (French *jambon,* Spanish *jamón*), chicken and/or seafood with rice, tomatoes and peppers (capsicums). Probably has links to *arroz con pollo* and *paella.*

Kale: A dark green, small-leafed vegetable similar to spinach, which can be substituted.

Lima beans: Originating from tropical America these white beans are similar to the butter bean (which is a good alternative) but tend to be smaller and slightly sweeter.

Molasses (black treacle): Molasses is the residue left when cane sugar is refined. It has a strong burnt toffee flavour.

Mustard greens: A cabbage-like plant with thick pale green stems and large green leaves. It has a slightly pungent, almost bitter taste. Can be used fresh or pickled.

Okra (gumbo, lady's fingers): Originally from West Africa, this popular vegetable is found all over the American South. It is a green-ridged immature seed pod, about 2–4 inches/5–10 cm long, pointed at one end. The West African word for okra, *n'gombo,* gave gumbo its name. Used for thickening and flavour in gumbos, soups and stews.

Peppers (capsicums): An essential ingredient in most Creole and Cajun dishes, peppers are used fresh or dried, whole or ground into powders. Fresh green, red or yellow peppers are used in almost every dish, and chillies – from fresh jalapeños to dried, ground cayenne – provide much of the heat. Tabasco and other hot pepper sauces are made from fermented cayenne peppers and salt.

Persimmon: A soft orangey-red fruit with blotchy skin and delicious soft flesh. A good and more readily available alternative is the Sharon fruit which was developed in Israel but has had the seeds and, sadly, the astringency bred out of it.

Radicchio: A type of Italian chicory. Similar in appearance to a very small lettuce, it has beautiful deep red leaves with cream veins. Crisp, slightly bitter leaves make a colourful addition to any salad.

Red bean (kidney bean): Readily available dried or canned.

Roux: The base of much of Louisiana cooking, this blend of oil and flour flavours and colours many dishes. Roux is usually cooked in a frying pan to the requisite colour, aromatic vegetables are then added and the mixture is used to flavour and thicken a soup or gumbo. See "Making a Roux" (page 8).

Savoy Cabbage: Similar to the common or round head cabbage, but with more wrinkled leaves.

Shucked Oysters: are shelled oysters.

Sweet potato (sometimes known as brown-skinned yam): A root vegetable that is pinkish red and resembles a large, swollen carrot. The flesh is more like swede in texture than the common potato and has a surprisingly sweet flavour.

Turnip greens: The turnip, a root vegetable, is a member of the mustard family. The root part of the vegetable will keep fresh in the refrigerator for weeks, but the leaves or "greens" will only keep for about two days. Turnip greens can be served in salads or cooked as for spinach.

INDEX

prawn remoulade 14
prawn salad, Creole 80
prawn stew 37
prawns
    barbecued 17
    boiled in beer 36
    in tomato lime chilli sauce 16
prime rib, blackened 59
pudding, bread 106
pudding
    Creole rice 104
    persimmon 107

quail, braised 55

rabbit
    and andouille gumbo 25
    in sauce piquante 52
red bean, bourbon and molasses soup 27
red beans and rice 73
rice
    dirty 74
    green 75
rice pudding, Creole 104
rice salad, Cajun 81
roux 8

salad
    Cajun rice 81
    Creole chicken or prawn 80
    duck cracklins and bitter greens 85
    pickled corn and okra 83
    pickled pepper and prawn 82
    potato, Plaquemine Parish 86
    spinach and hot pepper pecan 79
    wilted greens 84
sauce
    Cajun barbecue 65
    Cajun basting 64
    Creole 43
    meuniére with hot pepper pecans 45
    piquante 51
    remoulade 13
    tomato lime chilli 15
    whisky 105
sea bass, grilled, with Diable butter 42